You're NOT My Mom!

Confessions of a Formerly "Wicked" Stepmother

Kali and Elizabeth Schnieders

NAVPRESS®

BRINGING TRUTH TO LIFE

OUR GUARANTEE TO YOU

We believe so strongly in the message of our books that we are making this quality guarantee to you. If for any reason you are disappointed with the content of this book, return the title page to us with your name and address and we will refund to you the list price of the book. To help us serve you better, please briefly describe why you were disappointed. Mail your refund request to: NavPress, P.O. Box 35002, Colorado Springs, CO 80935.

The Navigators is an international Christian organization. Our mission is to reach, disciple, and equip people to know Christ and to make Him known through successive generations. We envision multitudes of diverse people in the United States and every other nation who have a passionate love for Christ, live a lifestyle of sharing Christ's love, and multiply spiritual laborers among those without Christ.

NavPress is the publishing ministry of The Navigators. NavPress publications help believers learn biblical truth and apply what they learn to their lives and ministries. Our mission is to stimulate spiritual formation among our readers.

Schnieders, Kali.
  You're not my mom : confessions of a formerly "wicked" stepmother /
Kali and Elizabeth Schnieders.
    p. cm.
Includes bibliographical references.
ISBN 1-57683-793-9
1. Stepmothers--Religious life. 2. Christian women--Religious life.
I. Schnieders, Elizabeth. II. Title.
BV4529.18.S36 2005
248.8'431--dc22
                    2004021192

Printed in the United States of America

1 2 3 4 5 6 7 8 9 10 / 09 08 07 06 05

FOR A FREE CATALOG OF NAVPRESS BOOKS & BIBLE STUDIES,
CALL 1-800-366-7788 (USA) OR 1-800-839-4769 (CANADA)

In memory of our mothers,
Betty and Annette.
And in honor of all women
who strive to raise another mother's child.

And for Larry,
the best husband and father two women could share.

With special thanks to Bruce, Rachelle, Jodi, Penny, Susan, Ann,
and the Lunch Bunch.

We are grateful to all who prayed us safely through
the troubled waters.

And we are grateful to God, who worked
everything together for good.

Contents

Introduction

When our family tied the knot, it nearly strangled us like a noose! Guilt, competition, and jealousy plagued us. Hot tempers and angry words often characterized our interactions. Disillusionment with our unmet expectations knocked each of us off balance. The complexity of building a healthy stepfamily was shocking and regularly threatened to destroy the love we were trying to build.

If this sounds uncomfortably familiar to you, take heart. We are living proof that no matter how splintered a family may be, holding tightly to God, persevering through trials, and learning from mistakes lets hope and harmony emerge in ways that never seemed possible.

Stepmothers often enter marriage *in love* with a man and then *learn to love* his children. We're blissfully unaware of the treacherous trail ahead: moments of pure joy alternating with frustration, confusion, and the temptation to give up. It's baffling. We have every intention of creating a happy family but are perplexed to find joy so elusive.

Statistics indicate that many stepfamilies, unable to overcome the extreme challenge, throw in the towel. It's a sad situation for everyone, causing even more grief for the children, who've already suffered so much loss in their lives. We wrote this book in hopes of helping stepfamilies avoid that fate. Even more, we want to encourage stepmothers to hang in there when the going gets tough. Make room for God to work. He promises a glorious opportunity for all of us—parents and children—to grow in unexpected ways.

Along with Larry (Elizabeth's father and Kali's husband), we have been a stepfamily for fourteen years. Much of the heartache we endured is common in stepfamilies. We don't offer our experience as the blueprint for family success, but we know that others can learn from our blunders. Our story has a happy ending, but along the way, we made just as many bad decisions as good ones. So this is not a how-to manual; rather, it's a story about one stepmother and daughter who have united in the face of difficulty, persevered against the odds, and developed a deep and loving bond. We learned the hard way, but we want to spare you some of that. If our story illuminates what not to do and helps you understand some of your own tough situations, our goal will have been accomplished.

Let us reassure you that there has never been a mother who knew less about child rearing than Kali. She was more career girl than mommy material—a hard-charging, job-focused perfectionist who never even babysat in high school. Meanwhile, Elizabeth was a whirlwind of activity who demanded constant attention and lived with the deluded notion that "real" mothers all bake Martha Stewart–style cookies with one hand while sewing mother-daughter dresses with the other.

Our family suffered for many years from the residual sadness and anger over the death of Larry's first wife and Elizabeth's mother, Annette, five years prior to our wedding. This lingering pain is normal and affects virtually every stepfamily. Whether the original family was broken up due to death or divorce, the children still suffer (and being only human, so do the adults involved). Stepmothers, by definition, are always dealing with a "real" mother somewhere out there—one the kids not only love but also idealize. If you find your family's equilibrium toppled by memories of and comparisons to the birth mom, take comfort in the fact that we've been there! Although it's one of the toughest issues stepmothers face, it can be surmounted with love, patience, and the grace of God.

Countless times we were each tempted to shout, "Enough already—this is never going to work!" Thankfully, we didn't listen to those voices; we listened to God instead. Our family learned some valuable lessons on our journey: God is still in the miracle business, and turning hearts from hatred to love is as easy for Him as turning water to wine.

Kali and Elizabeth

✳ *Chapter One* ✳

One Goose Step at a Time

Marriage is to be held in honor among all.
—Hebrews 13:4

I paused in the midst of my own wedding preparations to watch our flower girl. Emerald silk and velvet twirled in a blur as eight-year-old Elizabeth playfully danced in circles. The full skirt billowed away from her delicate frame with a swooshing sound as the crinoline petticoat fluttered with every movement—and her movement was considerable.

Hoping to postpone the inevitable scuffing of her new black patent leather shoes until after the ceremony, I contemplated how I could distract Elizabeth into a less active frame of mind. *Perhaps my frame of mind needs a calming adjustment too,* I thought, just as the wreath of flowers that adorned her French braid slipped down over one of her eyes. I reached out to adjust it. Elizabeth recoiled, her usual response to my touch.

"Don't you want me to fix it for you, honey?" I asked, anticipating her answer and yet hoping she might accept my offer this time.

"I can do it myself," Elizabeth informed me, looking at me out of the corner of her eye while she adjusted her headpiece.

In a mere matter of moments, our lives would be joined forever. Elizabeth and I were devoted to the same man—her father—and today the three of us would become a family. Our hopes were high, our emotions mixed, and our anxieties palpable.

This is a big day. It's natural for her to be a little edgy, I thought, trying to reassure my fearful heart with an encouraging explanation for her hands-off attitude.

Almost two years earlier, my relationship with Elizabeth had begun with promise when Larry planned a Fourth of July outing for the three of us. As the day progressed from parade to picnic to fireworks display, she seemed to warm up to the idea of me tagging along on *their* date.

It had been more than three years since Elizabeth's mother died, and the father-daughter bond was close and tight. I wondered if she could even make room for an outsider, but as the sun set and the colorful explosions filled the sky, Elizabeth snuggled into my lap as naturally as my little dog, Pandy, had done each evening for the past fifteen years.

Tender, almost protective feelings toward this little stranger had welled up inside me—emotions I had never known before this moment. *Is this what it feels like to be a mother?* I wondered.

My relationship with Larry was far too premature for such questions. Still, the warmth of Elizabeth's small hand on my forearm and the gentleness of her breathing as she nestled against me lured my mind to ponder the prospect. The moment was charming, but it didn't last long.

Just as unexpectedly as she had gotten there, Elizabeth squirmed out from my lap and into Larry's arms. She said nothing. The look she shot in my direction as she fled my lap seemed to communicate, "This is where I belong. His are the only arms I can trust."

Because Larry lived in Topeka and I lived more than an hour away in Kansas City, our courtship progressed slowly but steadily. Initially our dates were romantic dinners for two mingled with business outings that welcomed escorts but not offspring. Occasionally, Larry arranged kid-friendly events, such as picnics and movies, to include Elizabeth, but often she stayed with Grandma and Grandpa Schnieders while Larry and I went out. As our courtship progressed, so did Elizabeth's unspoken yet clearly communicated disdain for my deepening relationship with her father:

Yuck! Daddy is holding Kali's hand again. This is getting to be a habit. She's wrecking everything! Here, Dad, hold my hand instead.

Why do I have to sit in the backseat when Kali's in the car? I can't even reach the radio knobs from here. Even sitting on top of Daddy's briefcase, I'm too short to see out the front window. Everything's changed since she came along.

And those restaurants she likes are nasty. McDonald's not good enough for you, Kali? I don't want to go to Tippin's. I hate Tippin's. They don't have anything I like to eat at all. Why does she get to pick where we eat all the time? I hate her.

Why do we have to go to Kansas City so much? I never get to play with my best friend, Amanda, on the weekends now. Amanda's mother isn't married. Why can't Dad date her? She's already a great mother, and Amanda and I could be together all the time if we were sisters. Kali doesn't know anything about kids; I'd have to teach her how to be a mother. And Kali's stupid mutt, Pandy, tries to eat all my stuff. I'll have to make a Pandy protector just to keep my toys safe. This stinks!

"She seems angry, Larry. Am I doing something wrong?" I asked the question so often that it seemed like a mantra that emanated from my lips whenever Elizabeth was with us.

Larry's response was frequently the same: "Oh, I think she's just tired. She gets a little cranky when she's tired. We all do."

Well, we all don't kick something or someone when we're tired, I thought. But because I was falling in love, I let it go. Of course, now I know that children struggling to cope with a parent's new relationship often do lash out in frustration (and the "intruder" makes a handy target). But at the time, I viewed such manners through parentally challenged lenses and could only interpret Elizabeth's conduct as "spoiled brat" behavior. Sadly, I failed to read the pain she hid behind her anger.

Time passed, and my relationship with Larry blossomed, but my plot in the garden of Elizabeth's heart seemed continually overgrown with weeds. Then, at the point that my doubts had climbed higher than Jack's proverbial beanstalk, she would do something endearing.

"Hey Kali, ya wanna shop at my store?" Elizabeth's call came from my living room.

Larry was in the front yard resealing my driveway. *This man is as handy as a pocket on a shirt,* I thought as I watched him slather black gooey stuff onto my cracked driveway. That morning, Larry had arrived with "driveway shoes" and a willingness to tackle this manly chore that left me clueless. After monumental verbal affirmation, I left Larry to his sticky work while I went inside to make some lunch.

"Sure, I'd love to see your store," I called back to Elizabeth as I laid down the peanut-buttered knife.

I wandered into the living room to find the toys she'd brought from Topeka spread into a retail configuration. She had arranged several items, including her little purse, several colorful hair bows, and everything else from her suitcase. The young entrepreneur had even confiscated things from my closet and offered them for sale.

Must be a resale shop, I chuckled to myself, but my audible response was much more positive. "Wow, this is an awesome gift shop," I gushed, sincerely impressed that Elizabeth's artful flair for merchandise display had managed to tempt me with my own clothes!

"I noticed you looking at the hair bows. Do you have children?" Elizabeth asked with all of the professionalism of a personal shopper. "This pink bow is very popular with little girls. How old is your daughter?"

"I don't really have a child of my own," I said, "but I have a special little friend who is wild about pink."

"Oh, then she'll *love* this!" Elizabeth exclaimed, matching up the hair bow with her little pink purse. "All little girls want My Little Pony purses. Will this be cash or credit?" She concluded efficiently, "Your total is only ten dollars."

"Oh, I don't think I have that much cash on me. Better make it credit," I said. I saw where this was going, but I grasped the concept a little late. I was in over my head with the store game. Elizabeth was fully expecting me to shell out real dollars for this bogus purchase. *She's cute* and *smart,* I thought.

I opened my invisible purse and drew out an equally invisible Visa card. She grinned her impish grin, pretended to swipe my imaginary card in her air machine, and added the sound effects with gusto: "*Zip, zip.*"

Then she leaned in closer to me and said under her breath, "Of course, I'm just pretending to accept credit cards, Kali. You'll have to pay cash later when you have the money. I'll trust you for it."

Just then, Larry came in for a break. "What are my two girls up to?" he asked.

I described the game we'd been playing and showed Larry my purchases. "Quite a salesgirl we have here," Larry winked.

He beamed at the seven-year-old con artist, not realizing his daughter had genuine financial expectations at the conclusion of the store game. I pulled him aside and whispered, "Larry, she's got me for ten dollars, and I think she's playing for keeps! What should I do?"

I was grateful when Larry came to the rescue.

"Just follow my lead," he whispered back. Then he turned to Elizabeth. "This store game sounds fun! Can I play?"

"Sure," she said.

I turned to leave. "You'll love this store, Larry! Why don't you do a little shopping and pay the bill while I get lunch on?"

Larry browsed and enjoyed the game awhile and then plopped another hair bow on top of my items. "Okay, miss, how much is the total bill?"

Elizabeth calculated and proclaimed, "That will be ten dollars and fifty cents, sir!"

Larry reached in his wallet, pulled out imaginary money, and said with a wink, "Here's eleven. You may keep the change as a tip for great service."

Elizabeth protested, "Now, Dad, we're talking real dollars here, not pretend money."

I was right! I thought, listening from the kitchen. That little squirt in pink tennis shoes was trying to bamboozle me out of ten bucks. When I was Elizabeth's age, ten dollars was a year's allowance; it was 365 made beds! I'm glad I didn't fall prey to her game of extortion. I'm not interested in purchasing her affection like a melon at the market.

"Honey, we don't play games for real money," Larry explained. "However, I was planning on us all going to a movie later. How's that sound?"

"All right, but I get to pick the movie."

I knew that Kali would worm her way out of paying me the money she owed me. She's nothing like the other women Dad dated, who always brought me expensive gifts, like the one who even gave me a real pearl necklace. What does Kali do? She rips me off! Oh, she'll pay for this.

Elizabeth was very cool toward me for the rest of the evening. Unwittingly, I had done damage to an already fragile relationship.

The next morning, I wandered into the bathroom to get ready for work. I flipped my makeup mirror from the regular to the magnifying side, thinking it was odd for it to be out of position.

"Eeeeeeeeeeek!" I screamed at the top of my lungs. Pandy came running to my defense. There on the mirror was a small gray lizard with a very wiggly tail. I fell back against the bathroom door and sighed with relief when I realized that it was a rubber toy attached to my makeup mirror by a suction cup and that the tail movement was merely an elastic appendage that bounced to and fro because I had jostled the mirror. It was *not* a woman-eating reptile. Pandy cocked his head and arched his ears.

"That little rascal," I said with a laugh (when my heart regained its beat). I was delighted and amused by Elizabeth's practical joke. I interpreted her little gag as sweet and clever. It was something I might do to someone I cared for a great deal. I didn't realize that the hidden lizard was no gesture of endearment—it was a declaration of war.

Not long after the lizard incident, Larry proposed and I accepted. We agreed to tell Elizabeth after church on Sunday, and I wondered how she would handle the news. After the church service, we stopped in at Wendy's, knowing this was her favorite dining establishment. Elizabeth requested a kid's meal: a hamburger, fries, Coke, a Frosty, and a toy. She loved Wendy's because their free-refill policy allowed her to top off her Coke without limitation. Father and daughter always scoffed at my objection to the sugar overdose, so this particular day I kept my mouth shut. I figured I had plenty of time to correct unhealthy eating habits down the road.

Larry had already discussed the idea of our marriage privately with Elizabeth. Nevertheless, I was quite nervous when he began to speak: "Honey, Kali and I have been talking about us all becoming a family. What would you think about that?" he asked.

The child had an absolute talent for keeping us in suspended agony. Elizabeth first took a looooong draw from her Frosty until the straw made a loud slurping sound as it sucked in air. She set down her cup, wiped her hands and mouth with her napkin, looked me square in the eye, and asked in a matter-of-fact tone, "Well, can I call you Mother?"

Tears welled up in my eyes. For the time I'd known Elizabeth, she was either kicking me under the table, making fun of me in some way, or launching an "I hate you" in my direction. *Could I have heard correctly? Does Elizabeth really want to call me Mother?* I was tempted to pinch myself to see if I'd dozed off and entered a dream.

I'd never been more surprised or more delighted by a single question, except for the night when Larry proposed. I hadn't seen either question coming, and I was equally elated by both offers.

"Of course you can call me Mother, honey. I'd be honored," I gushed as the emotion of the moment overwhelmed me.

Over the next few months, Elizabeth tried the "mother" label on me for size, but she ultimately decided it didn't fit. No matter. I'd grown accustomed to hearing her call me Kali, and her inclination to see me as her mother is what really counted.

About six months after Elizabeth had determined my proper nomenclature, we were all heading down the aisle toward a vow. Elizabeth and I made quite a pair—I in my satin gown and she in her crinoline petticoat. I decided to make another stab at connection, so I said, "Elizabeth, I was thinking that because today is a special occasion, you might like to wear a little of my pink lipstick."

Elizabeth's glare melted immediately into a smile. I knew by her reaction I'd hit the jackpot, so I got out the lipstick, removed the top, and then bent down and placed my hand under her chin. I gently lifted her face and dabbed a light coat of Pink Blossom color to her lips. Our eyes met, and in that moment, a measure of love was communicated.

Then I pressed my lips together, demonstrating the proper technique for spreading the color evenly across the lips and thus offering Elizabeth a visual image to mimic. She performed a flawless imitation.

"You look beautiful, Elizabeth. Now let's all go get married," I whispered.

Elizabeth nodded her head, and we made our way down the hall toward the chapel, where her father, the wedding party, and our guests were waiting. The music gave the signal for Elizabeth to scatter the rose petals from her little basket and glide down the aisle ahead of me.

Well, maybe having a mother won't be such a bad thing. Dad was great to be a room mother at school, but he was the only man in the room. And Kali's beauty pageant experience will probably come in handy because I bet she knows a few cool makeup tricks that most mothers have never even heard of before!

Maybe we'll shop together on the weekends, and she can sew on my Girl Scout badges and even bake me chocolate chip cookies. Only problem is, Kali will always think she's the queen. I'll just have to come up with ways to be the center of attention, starting right now!

Nothing could have prepared me for what happened next. Elizabeth abandoned the delicate procedure we had practiced so thoroughly during rehearsal the night before. She suddenly stiffened her little arms and legs and then thrust them out in time to the music, thus proclaiming our new family union and a moment of holy matrimony with a military-style goose-step march!

Elizabeth proved to be full of surprises, and from the wedding day forward, I sensed my goose was cooked. Elizabeth had been the star of her father's life for years, and in her eyes, my arrival on the scene meant she had a competitor for center stage. Both of us wanted Larry's attention, and both of us had competitive streaks in our personalities. Had I realized that a "love triangle" like this is not unusual in stepfamilies, the next few years of our lives would have been far, far easier. Fortunately, though, we weren't in this alone. God was with us—and nothing took Him by surprise.

If Only I Had Known . . .

- Competition for the leading-lady role is commonplace.
- Power struggles are common in all types of families, not just stepfamilies.

What I Would Have Done Differently

I wish I'd been able to avoid becoming engaged in competition. As the adult in the situation, it was my responsibility to rise above the question of whom Larry loved the most and instead focus on reassuring Elizabeth that she was loved—by her father, her mother, and now me. I might have told her more often what I liked about her and why I was glad to have her in my life. Maybe she'd have opened up to me more easily had I said things like, "I don't know much about children, but I enjoy learning about you. Tell me how you feel about . . ."

It's easy to get drawn in by the child's efforts to create a power struggle. Elizabeth positioned herself against me in the attempt to be tops with Larry. She also pitted Larry and I against each other. Rather than fighting for my place in the family, I could have actively encouraged the continued father/daughter bond, letting Elizabeth know that it was not my intention to "steal" her dad's love.

Reflecting on Your Own Family

- In what ways has competition been apparent in your relationship with your stepchildren?
- How do you think your stepchildren felt about your marriage to their dad, and how have you responded to those feelings?
- How have you dealt with your stepchildren's needs to be first place in their father's life?
- What could you do to minimize competition in your family?

* Chapter Two *

Stepping over the Threshold and into the Fire

Unless the LORD builds the house, the stepmom labors in vain.
—PSALM 127:1 (PARAPHRASED)

"Okay, Elizabeth, hurry up and finish your lunch. Your dad and Kali will be home from their honeymoon in about two hours!" Grandma Schnieders announced.

A few months before our wedding, Larry and Elizabeth had moved from their former home in Topeka to our new home in Lawrence and had already begun fine-tuning their new environment. We figured Elizabeth might need a jump-start on adjusting to her new third-grade class before I arrived on the scene. Larry's parents were delighted to come to Lawrence and watch Elizabeth so she could continue her schoolwork without interruption while we honeymooned. "You've got to get your room spick-and-span because Sarge will be doing a thorough inspection!" Grandma often joked about herself being a strict sergeant who did white-glove inspections of little girls' rooms and gave merit awards for a job well done. The old gag usually worked because Elizabeth loved working for any kind of a prize, but today she rolled her eyes and slowed her eating further. She moved the French fries around on her plate, drawing circles with them in the ketchup.

If Grandma thinks she can con me with that sergeant stuff, she can forget it! I like my room just the way it is. At least I used to like my room before I had to move here. I can't believe Dad went off with Kali and left me for a whole week. It seems like months! I miss him so much. I miss our polka dancing in the living room and SpaghettiOs for supper, and most of all, I miss him reading to me at bedtime. Grandma and Grandpa try, but they don't read it the same way as my dad.

"Come on, Pokey. You want Grandpa to help you with those fries?" Grandpa Schnieders asked, trying to do his part in speeding up the process.

"What's the big deal about a clean room?" Elizabeth whined. "Dad doesn't make me clean my room. Why should *you* care? I'm going outside."

Elizabeth ran from the table, leaving her dishes. She bolted out the back door and into the woods behind the golf course (her favorite cooling-off and "thinking things over" place) before Grandma could catch her. But before too long, Elizabeth was back, heading straight for her room without a word to anyone. About an hour later, she appeared at the top of the stairs and called out, "Okay, Sergeant, ready for inspection!"

Grandma was a little surprised at Elizabeth's sudden about-face, but she wasn't entirely unfamiliar with her granddaughter's unpredictable behavior that often flip-flopped without explanation. Grandma climbed the stairs and gushed over the marvelous cleaning job. "Grandpa, come see!" she called. "You won't even recognize this room. Why, it's clean enough to pass Sarge's white-glove test. I'd say this calls for ice cream!"

Elizabeth beamed and headed for the car with a renewed spring in her step.

As the ice cream eaters returned from their outing and pulled into the driveway, Larry and I cruised toward home listening to the song "I've Had the Time of My Life." *Could have been the theme song for our honeymoon,* I thought as we both sang along.

I had always imagined our arrival at home to be as romantic as a movie scene, with my dashing husband swooping me into his strong arms and carrying me over the threshold. *Then* we would greet the family. But the sight of Elizabeth and the in-laws climbing out of their car ended my daydream.

"Daaaaaaad!" Elizabeth squealed her excitement as Larry's car door swung open. She flew into her daddy's arms like a homing pigeon returning to the safety of her coop. "What'd you bring me?" she chirped.

"Oh, I think there's something you might like in one of those suitcases," Larry teased.

I greeted them congenially, masking my disappointment about the magical "threshold moment." (I realize my fantasy was unrealistic, but I'm a sucker for romance, and I was clinging to the dreamy-eyed notion that courtship gallantry would extend into matrimony.) It was slowly beginning to sink in that I had married two people, not one.

I smiled and turned to Elizabeth. "Hi there. How 'bout a hug?" I asked, tickling her side gently as we all walked into the house.

Elizabeth swatted my hand away as though it were a pesky fly and ignored my question. She squirmed in Larry's arms, making it difficult for him to hold on to her. "Dad, I want to go see Amanda."

"Whoa, we just walked in, Elizabeth. Kali and I have to unpack and do a few things around here. We can't be driving all the way to Topeka today. We've got to go to Kansas City and move the rest of Kali's things and then pick up Pandy from the kennel."

Elizabeth wriggled out of Larry's arms and stomped her little foot. "No, Dad, I've been waiting *forever* for you to get home. I'm going to see Amanda today!" she said, changing it from a request to a demand. Her formerly cute voice escalated into a shrieking siren, and our homecoming moment turned into a good old-fashioned, mega-volume, bawling, kicking temper tantrum. "I want to see Amanda right now!" she screamed, loud enough for Amanda to hear her in Topeka.

I stood stunned, my mouth gaping open, revealing my children-should-be-seen-but-not-heard upbringing. My in-laws shuffled their feet in embarrassment while Larry tried his best to console and quiet Elizabeth. She screamed all the louder and began writhing on the floor.

Larry said tenderly, "Now, Elizabeth, this is no way to act. I'm so happy to be home and to be with you. Grandma and Grandpa are leaving soon. You don't want to spoil their nice visit, do you? We'll talk about seeing Amanda next weekend if you're on your best behavior this week."

Larry quickly rummaged through his suitcase to pull out the gifts we'd bought and handed boxes to Grandma and Grandpa. "Elizabeth," he tantalized, "if you don't stop crying I can't give you your present from Hawaii." He held up a pretty gold box. Shaking it, he pretended to listen for a rattle.

Elizabeth calmed momentarily as Grandma and Grandpa opened their boxes containing the gifts we'd selected. They looked adorable as they held the colorful Hawaiian shirts up to their chests and smiled broadly.

Our eight-year-old fashion plate loved clothes, so she excitedly grabbed the box from Larry's hands and pulled out a hot-pink floral dress. She threw it on the floor in disgust. The wailing resumed, and Elizabeth ran to her room, shrieking as she went, "I don't want that stupid dress. I don't want to live in Lawrence in this creepy *Star Wars* house. I *want* to go see Amanda!"

I don't know why Dad had to marry Kali, and why did we have to move to Lawrence? Things are never going to be the same now that she's moving in and bringing all her furniture-from-another-planet with her. I mean, who ever heard of a chair you're not allowed to sit in! Worst of all, I hardly ever get to see Amanda anymore, and boy do I have a lot to tell her! I hate going to school without her. I don't have anybody to pass secret notes to in class or swing with on the tire swing at recess. I'm just the "new kid" for everyone to ignore. Kali and Dad say I should be able to make friends easily. Of course, I can't make any friends here because they all think I live in a weird outer-space house. All of our old things are gone—even my mother's dishes! I hate it here. I hate my life!

Larry turned to his folks, smiled, and summed up the entire scene with one sentence: "She's probably tired."

Tired! I thought. *She's behaving like an ungrateful, demanding, spoiled little snot! This problem requires a bigger fix than a nap!*

Grandma caught my eye and whispered, "We're so glad you're home. It's been like this off and on ever since we arrived. I think she pines for her friend Amanda, and I know she missed Larry terribly while you were gone. We battled every night at bedtime. She simply wouldn't mind me no matter what I did."

Something is certainly tormenting Elizabeth to prompt such a dramatic scene, I thought. Missing Amanda, moving away from her old home—it was becoming clear how much Elizabeth had left behind when she and Larry moved to Lawrence. Now she was trying to cope with a new stepmother as well. It was obvious Elizabeth was struggling, but at the time, I had no clue how deep her pain really was.

Early on, Larry and I had agreed that the best way to get our marriage off on sound footing was to change surroundings rather than try to plug me into their former life. Larry understood why it wouldn't seem right for me to move into a love nest fashioned by his first wife's loving hands. This would also settle the design dilemma—I loved modern design, while Annette (Elizabeth's mother) had traditional taste. So together, Larry and I designed a beautiful new home—my dream house but Elizabeth's nightmare.

The location we chose was ideal for Larry and me but less so for Elizabeth. Lawrence was midway between Kansas City (where I worked) and Topeka (where Larry worked). The location allowed me to keep my sales position with a well-respected furniture manufacturer *and* furnish our home at a hefty discount. Elizabeth would have to change schools, but we figured that because she was a socially outgoing child with a resilient spirit, she would be fine—after all, she'd already moved several times due to corporate transfers.

Once the location was selected, it seemed logical to pack away the china and heirlooms for Elizabeth and hold a "getting-married garage sale" to sell the traditional furnishings that would look out of place with our décor. I never imagined that an eight-year-old would object. I hoped she would see my sleek design concepts as exciting, fresh, even hip! But my contemporary taste stuck out like a petunia in the rose garden of our traditional neighborhood, and our new-kid-on-the-block was not enamored with the distinction.

Not only was embarrassment an issue, Elizabeth's overwhelming loss had totally escaped me: she had been the lady of the house for five years in a home full of cherished memories of her mother. Now here she was in a place that felt nothing like home. Neither Larry nor I guessed how distressing it would be for Elizabeth to be wrenched from Annette's environment and thrown into mine. Somehow it never dawned on me that a child might be attached to a particular décor not solely because of taste but because it represented "home" and her lost mother.

As a new wife, I was simply focused on creating an environment where a loving family could flourish, and like all wives, I wanted our home to carry my own personal touch. But I was so inept at relating to children that I never even tried to open the door to Elizabeth's emotions—partially because the chief emotion I saw her reveal was anger, and I didn't want to invite any more of that!

My only experience with children came from my own childhood. When my parents divorced, my mom did not probe deeply into my emotions. My feelings were largely swept over, and I guess I was unwittingly repeating a pattern I didn't even realize was flawed. My mother had managed to communicate that emotions were to be worked out on one's own—or in today's vernacular, "Get over it."

If a birth mother could botch something so badly, I suppose I was entitled to a few mistakes. Yet I wish I had asked Elizabeth to tell me more about her feelings over the décor, the house, and the move. I thought her put-downs of my furniture and artwork were simply another way to reject me. Because she picked out the things for her own bedroom, I figured her personal needs had been addressed. I have often wondered how our relationship might have been different if I'd taken the time to probe a little further about not only the furniture but also how she felt about having to move. Even if our decisions had remained the same, at least she would have known I cared enough to listen.

I began to wonder if we'd done irreparable harm by adding relocation to the compromises we'd all have to make in living together as a family. To say our family's adjustment to marriage was stressful is like saying a hurricane is a bad hair day. We all enter relationships with expectations that are likely to go unmet. If the expectations aren't discussed in advance of the wedding vows, a power struggle can result. And when three people tie the knot, the tie that binds can quickly become a noose! If I had understood that fact, I might have eased some of our stress by sharing my own expectations openly and honestly before the marriage, particularly in the areas of parenting and domestic responsibility.

Larry was looking for me to lighten his load where Elizabeth's needs were concerned, but I had been expecting him to continue in the stellar hands-on parenting style I had come to admire—and depend upon. Elizabeth was not enamored with my increased involvement in her day-to-day routine. It seemed to me her expectations of having a stepmother in the house were for me to stay locked in a closet until summoned and then appear only to wash her clothes or buy her something.

I wanted a new mom, but Kali's not what I had in mind. I was better off when "Aunt" Ann looked after me while Dad was at work; at least she made great home-cooked suppers and taught me how to play the piano. I wish Dad could have married someone like her! Kali doesn't seem to be good for much that I can tell. She's always working at that stupid furniture company, and she acts like taking me to run errands is a big chore. Now I'm stuck with her!

Every day became a flurry of activity that set us all on edge. Larry's commute was about thirty minutes each way, while mine was closer to an hour with heavy traffic, thus subtracting nearly two hours from my amazingly shortened twenty-four-hour day. At one point, Larry even suggested that I consider quitting my job. That certainly would have eased the stress of our time crunch, but it didn't seem financially realistic at the time. And even though my boss was starting to take note of my slumping sales figures, my job was an oasis compared with a stay-at-home assignment caring for a child who detested me.

So for the meantime, I would cope with the long workdays and the commute. But when I finally arrived at home, it was time to cook! *What do you mean, what's for dinner? I hoped we'd be going out to eat!* I grumbled to myself, remembering all of those courtship candlelight dinners in nice restaurants. Besides, I didn't know how to cook! I had been a single, career-minded woman eating micro-meals. At least I had cookbooks. I'd never cracked one open except to look at the pictures, but I had them. "This sounds perfect," I said to Pandy. "*After Work Cookbook: Quick Meals in a Jiffy.*"

Flipping through the pages, I saw something that sounded tasty, and I even had most of the ingredients. *Yum. Three-cheese Mexican lasagna. Okay, I don't have pepperjack cheese, but I do have Swiss. I like Mexican and I love lasagna—tossing in a third culture can only improve the dish, right? Let's give it a whirl. How hard can this be?*

I set the table with the everyday dishes we'd received as wedding gifts and opened the window so a nice breeze would refresh us as we ate, fondly remembering the many nights we dated and dined alfresco. *The fresh air will set a nice atmosphere,* I thought as the timer announced that the food was ready. I called to my family, "Come and get it!"

"Down in a minute. I've got to get this checkbook to balance." Larry called out.

"Elizabeth, let's eat. Food is better when it's hot," I called out as cheerfully as I could muster. *With as much trouble as I've gone to for this dinner, they could at least come before it's cold!*

Larry came down to the table while I drummed my fingers on the countertop waiting for Elizabeth.

Larry sat down, eyeballed my curious-looking creation, and simply asked, "And what exactly do you call this dish?"

I sat down and responded with pride, "Mexican lasagna."

Elizabeth slammed the window closed. "I don't like the wind blowing while I eat," she announced.

"Yes, that probably is better. Thanks, Elizabeth," Larry chimed in.

You could have heard my eyes roll a block away. *Larry loved the breeze before* she *started whining about it.*

Elizabeth wriggled into her chair and sniffed a forkful of lasagna. "I'm not eating *this.*"

Before the "Yes, you are, young lady" could escape from my mouth, Larry took his first bite. I could tell by his expression that this Mexican lasagna wasn't going to win any Betty Crocker awards. I tasted it myself and quickly decided I'd be lucky if my dish didn't get me arrested for attempted murder.

"This is disgusting!" Elizabeth snapped, running to the kitchen. She poured herself a bowl of Cocoa Puffs, headed for the loft, and plopped in front of the television.

Mexican lasagna—oh, brother. So much for coming home from school to a batch of hot chocolate chip cookies fresh from the oven. Kali probably can't even pour milk! She's still at work when I get home anyway. What a dork of a stepmother she's turning out to be. Yesterday I caught her "sewing" my Girl Scout badges to my sash with Velcro. No way am I asking her to be room mother now. She'd probably poison my friends—that is if I had any friends. I miss my mommy so much.

The following night, the dinner I prepared was not much better, and by the end of the week, Elizabeth announced in self-defense, "From now on, I'm cooking my own meals."

Each night, she would cruise the kitchen, make an insulting comment about the meal I was preparing, and begin making her own meal. Her "cooking" mostly consisted of elbowing me out of her way and removing my things from the microwave to nuke a frozen pizza. I guess that makes us even in the cooking department, but I really was trying to learn the art of preparing healthy cuisine.

After about a week, I became concerned about Elizabeth's diet. "Larry, have you noticed what Elizabeth is calling 'dinner'? She's concocted some sort of entrée using Uncle Ben's instant white rice with a squirt of hot water. Her dinners consist entirely of undercooked rice, pizza, Cocoa Puffs, potato chips, and apples. That is not a healthy diet," I worried. "Children need vegetables, protein, and milk—lots of milk!"

We defaulted into frequent trips for fast-food, and on those nights, Larry reminded me that Elizabeth's kid's meal included meat (if you call cardboard hamburgers meat). "There's calcium in that Frosty, you know," he said emphatically.

"And I suppose a pickle counts as the five servings of fruits and vegetables she needs too?" I retorted. "Unless Doritos have recently been added as a Basic Food Group, that child is *not* properly nourished."

"Now Kali," Larry cautioned, "don't worry about her eating habits. I've been at this parenting thing for quite awhile. When Annette died, I was concerned about my ability to give Elizabeth proper nutrition, so I asked her pediatrician about it. He said, 'If you leave kids alone, their bodies will tell them what is missing, and they'll eat what they need.'"

"I suppose that might be true if a child didn't come home from school and eat an entire bag of chips and drink four Cokes before dinner!" I ranted.

But Larry didn't want to hear any more about her diet. My sensitivity meter was in double digits, and I wondered if Larry felt he had made a matrimonial mistake. I was starting to question the same thing.

"This is not what I signed up for, Pandy," I confided to my furry friend. I had imagined chatty family dinners where we would all discuss our day, followed by an evening of playing a nice board game together. Weeks of nightly strain at mealtime were taking a toll on us. Elizabeth was growing increasingly aggressive with verbal jabs at me, and I was growing more irritated myself.

The issues for a stepparent are complicated under the best of circumstances, but I was handicapped due to a missing "mommy gene"—the one that instills a conviction that without children, life is meaningless. My mother had the gene, so I guess it skipped a generation. I hoped I would eventually get the hang of being a mother. But Elizabeth hated me, and that is one thing she always communicated effectively.

"Elizabeth, that was uncalled for," my husband would say. But oh, how I longed to hear him announce a zero-tolerance policy and punctuate it by saying, "Kali may not be your mother, but she *is* my wife, and I expect you to treat her with respect!"

After a second or third offense, Larry usually laid out consequences for Elizabeth's inappropriate behavior. However, it seemed to me that Larry's "pride and joy" had a way of winding Daddy around her pinky, and I rarely felt the consequence was harsh enough to produce the desired result.

Regardless of what was said or done, the behavior didn't improve— it grew more offensive. My comments concerning Elizabeth aroused a papa bear's instinct to protect his child from an intruder's overbearing parental style. While it is true that a parent's first job is to protect the child (even from stepparents), the line between protection and put-down is extremely thin.

In reality, I spent more time with Elizabeth than Larry did. Needing some leverage to deal with Elizabeth's behavior, I wanted to be considered an equal partner on the parenting issues. But to Larry, I was more of an assistant coach who was overstepping her boundaries. Like so many stepparents, I had plenty of responsibility and no authority. As my role in our new family blurred, my questions mounted. Shall I be a friend, a mom, or some combination of both? Shall I voice my disagreement over parenting decisions, or take a backseat? What do I do with all of these feelings that seem to well up?

Then there was the issue of unconditional love.

From the moment the umbilical cord is severed, most parents begin falling head over heels in love with their baby. Mom and Dad agree that the child's needs are paramount. As the infant moves from newborn to toddler, giant love deposits are made daily into the parental bank account. Every smile, coo, and gurgle is amazing! By the time they hear the words "Mama and Dada," they're hooked. When hard times hit, they have the emotional reserves to deal with them because of the years of building up love.

But a stepparent entering the scene begins with an empty love account and from the get-go senses there is a run on the bank. Years may pass without any attempt to replenish the coffers (particularly when the child has been wounded, is angry about that loss, and has matured to "teen behavior" well before the proper time). All this may leave a stepmom asking, *Why must I act as though I have no needs, and why must I constantly bow to this miniature tyrant who kicks me one minute and then asks if her laundry is done the next?*

Deep down, even an inexperienced adult knows that the child's needs must come first. Therefore, guilt creeps in. "Love more and complain less," logic murmurs in our ears. But when we give and give without getting anything in return, even our best intentions can be challenged. Often, I felt that the smallest hint of appreciation would have been enough to help me want to keep giving.

So the tension mounted, and we all retreated to separate corners of the house to lament our unmet expectations.

Mommy, I miss you so much. Why did you have to leave me? I need you to come back, to tuck me in like you used to. I cry myself to sleep almost every night. I'm just not happy anymore without you; I don't think I'll be really happy ever again.

One night in my own hurt and confusion, I sought comfort in a devotional book and the comfy chair in our guest bedroom. I'd hardly settled into the cushions with the blanket over my lap when the tears began to roll. My own mother had crocheted that blanket for me, and as I felt its cozy warmth, I wished she were alive to reassure me and give me some motherly advice. Wrapped up in my pain, at the time it escaped me that Elizabeth and I might have been going through such similar struggles—missing the love and comfort of our mothers and not knowing if we were going to survive this.

I found myself staring at the ceiling, as if by looking hard enough I could see into heaven and obtain my mother's wisdom. "Mom, I don't know what to do. I thought a mother was what Elizabeth needed and a partner what Larry wanted. Yet no matter what I suggest, it seems

Larry doesn't want to hear it. I'm rarely taken seriously, and sometimes my motives are even questioned. Elizabeth definitely doesn't want my mothering. I don't know what she had in mind, but clearly I'm not a match. I may be living with people, but I'm lonelier than ever." I confided in my mother as though she were there in the room.

My soft tears turned to great sobs, and I took my complaint to a higher authority. "God, I need Your help. I'm in way over my head. I don't have any idea what I'm doing. I can't seem to make Jell-o, much less a casserole. I only know how to make my way in the corporate world, and those skills are woefully inadequate for this job. I made a promise on my wedding day, not only to them but also to You. I don't want to go back on my promises, but I've gotten wrapped up in a ball of twine that I can't untangle. Please help me."

It's hard to explain what happened next. A calm washed over me like a cool, refreshing rain. I felt a strong sense of reassurance, almost as though God were placing His hand upon my shaking shoulder. I dried my eyes and opened the devotional book on my lap to the reading for that day. I wept again when I saw the words printed on the page, but this time they were tears of joy.

> "Why art thou cast down, O my soul?" (Psalm 42:5). "Why?" It is good to get to the bottom of our troubles and our griefs. Get to the very bottom. To understand their cause is well on the way to their cure. . . .
>
> When the psalmist put the question to his soul, he discovered the cause for his deep grief. He found the trouble not so much in the severity of the conditions around him as in the darkness that pervaded his own soul. He had lost sight of God. . . .
>
> His "uplook" was obscured by his "outlook."[1]

It was true! In my well-meaning but misguided attempts to be Wonder Woman at work and Martha Stewart at home, I was so overwhelmed that any notion of turning to God for help hadn't even bleeped across my radar screen.

While I didn't know a thing about children, God did, and what's more, He knew everything about this child He'd put in my path. He knew about knotted balls of twine. Better yet, He knew how they became knotted and what was necessary to untangle them. He was willing to share His wisdom; all I had to do was ask.

From that day forward, I knew I was not in this marriage alone unless I chose to be. I had made my vows before God on our wedding day. When I said, "I do," God said, "So do I." But I had left Him at the church like a forgotten wedding gift. No wonder I was struggling in my marriage: I was doing some mighty heavy lifting alone and with puny muscles. Yet thankfully, in my desperation, my spirit had cried out to heaven, and heaven was answering back. God was extending His loving, strong arms and offering to help lift my burden.

If Only I Had Known . . .

- People begin relationships with high expectations that will likely go unmet, and everyone must cope with some degree of disappointment.
- Talking about expectations and disappointments can diffuse some of the tension in a new stepfamily.

What I Would Have Done Differently

Because no one gets everything they want in any relationship, knowing and understanding what everyone expects is a great starting point for family discussions. I wish I'd known enough to discuss nitty-gritty details before the wedding—things like who would cook dinner and how Larry envisioned our partnership when it came to raising Elizabeth.

Even after the wedding, it would have been helpful to discuss expectations as we went along. If I'd asked Elizabeth what she'd expected from a stepmother versus what she got, I might have learned some interesting things! Initiating that type of conversation would have let her know that I cared about her feelings and took them into account when making decisions.

Negotiating expectations is part of the blending process. We each had our own needs, hopes, and wish lists. Our family's adjustment might have been easier if we'd each spoken up a little more about how our expectations were meshing with reality.

Reflecting on Your Own Family

- How have you dealt with the differences between your expectations for your new family and the reality?
- What expectations do you think your stepchildren had about your marriage to their father, and how might they have been disappointed?

- In what ways do your ideas of discipline differ from your husband's, and what have you done to increase cooperation and solidarity?
- What are some things you could do, starting now, to help your family cope with differing parenting styles and unmet expectations?

* Chapter Three *

Shocking Steps

You can teach kids what you know, but you will reproduce what you are.
—Dr. Forest Tennant

I walked with a spring in my step as I entered our kitchen from the garage. I chirped a cheery "Hellooooo-o, I'm hooooo-ome."

No response.

I jingled my keys as a greeting to Pandy. "Hi, Wonder Dog," I said, swinging my briefcase up to the kitchen counter with one hand and grabbing his leash with the other. I looked forward to this walk because the weather was warming, spring flowers were bursting forth all over the neighborhood, and walking always melted away the stress of a busy workday.

Pandy demonstrated his enthusiasm with a wagging tail and doggy smile. "People who say dogs don't smile have never seen *you*, my friend!" I said, trying to detangle my ankles from Pandy's leash as he wound himself around me all the more tightly. "Where's that rascal Elizabeth, huh?" I asked, scratching the fluffy topknot on his head.

Elizabeth and I had gotten off to a rough start that morning with one of our characteristic arguments, this time over a discussion about leotards.

"Kali, can you come home early today? The gymnastics leos are in, and I want to go pick some out before the best ones are gone," Elizabeth coaxed in her sweetest voice.

Her request for new leotards was perfectly reasonable, and as often as she wore them, it was nearly impossible for me to keep them washed and ready as needed. *It sure would come in handy to have a few spares on hand so we could avoid some of our leo-laundry panic scenes,* I thought.

However, I already had big plans for this night, the only evening in weeks that I didn't have an after-work commitment. I was in desperate need of downtime in an easy chair without having to go anywhere. During my single life, I saved errands for the weekend and therefore could relax after work, but with a child in school, the frantic pace of family life—with every night a new crisis—was starting to wear on me.

Because I usually beat Larry home by at least an hour, it seemed logical to Elizabeth that I should be the one to go out after a long day to pick up her "emergency" purchase. I usually gave in, and granted, on many occasions, she needed things for a school-related project. However, frequently the item was a want (not a need) that could wait until the weekend. If I declined the request, my status instantly changed from "stepmother" to "wicked stepmother." Nevertheless, tonight I was putting my foot down. We could simply postpone the shopping trip and check out the leotard stock tomorrow night, when we would already be out for the evening. If another gymnast got to the coolest leotard ahead of us, well, I could live with it this time.

Initially, gymnastics lessons had seemed like a great idea. Larry diligently followed the advice of Elizabeth's maternal grandfather, Doc Laaser, who summed up good parenting with a single principle: "If you keep them busy, you keep them out of trouble." If the goal is to keep a nine-year-old busy, gymnastics is the perfect solution. We were very busy.

From the day Elizabeth enrolled in gymnastics classes at the University of Kansas, we were hooked like a mackerel. Elizabeth was so captivated by the sport that a simple class or two would never satisfy her hunger, and with her natural talent for tumbling, the instructors continually pushed her toward competition. From the moment she saw a first-place medal, Elizabeth's eyes lit up, her perfectionism kicked into overdrive, and she was driven—she simply *had* to be the best. With the simple signing of a parental consent form, after-work and weekends quickly became committed to gymnastics.

I was dazed by this consuming devotion to what I mistakenly imagined as a child's pastime. When I was Elizabeth's age, the term *soccer mom* had not entered mainstream motherhood, and the most athletic thing nine-year-old girls did in my neighborhood was put swimsuits on their Barbies. I was taken aback by Elizabeth's practice schedule and its impact upon our family life. From 7 to 9 PM three nights a week, Larry and I sat in the bleachers reading the newspaper, doing paperwork, and keeping an eye on our twirling, tumbling daughter. I looked around the gym and learned that we were not alone—this appeared to be an epidemic! The other parents seemed to sit on the edge of their seats as though they were watching future Olympians in training.

Afterward, we usually cruised for fast-food on the way home and then collapsed from a day that had begun with the annoying buzz of a 5:30 AM alarm clock.

Ah, then came the weekends. We went to at least two gymnastics meets per month, and many involved out-of-town travel and an overnight stay. We would all pile in the car at the crack of dawn and speed off to a competition somewhere across the plains of Kansas. The meets lasted four or five hours, only fifteen minutes of which involved Elizabeth's direct participation.

It wasn't easy on a new marriage to rarely have a peaceful night at home, but we were trying to satisfy Elizabeth's constant craving for more time at the gym. After a good performance, Elizabeth would chat breezily and relive the moments that had resulted in her newest ribbons or medals. But if the performance had not been up to snuff (meaning anything less than perfect in her mind), Elizabeth would not exhibit the same grace in sportsmanship that she displayed while negotiating those uneven parallel bars. On those occasions, I held my tongue. Given Elizabeth's tendency toward self-recriminating, post-competition analysis, I knew my sincere compliments were likely to be rebuffed. She was so driven toward perfection that I soon learned silence was better than words.

As much as Kali gets on my nerves, I have to admit she never misses a meet. It's awesome to look up in the stands and see Dad and Kali giving me a thumbs-up. Even though she bugs me by complimenting something when I stink and don't win any ribbons, I guess I'm pretty lucky to have support from both of them. Some of the girls don't have that.

They crack me up with that video camera—they aren't exactly hi-tech parents. It's cool that they record my every move. It really helps me to watch the tape so I can improve for my next meet.

Watching Elizabeth perform was like watching magic. Being barely able to negotiate my way down a set of bleachers without stumbling, I admired her ability. A motherly pride blossomed into existence each time I watched her perform on the balance beam. She would glide along with the grace and elegance of a swan sailing across a pond and then explode into a powerful dismount.

Elizabeth's mother had been a college cheerleader at Kansas State University, a fact that Larry brought up frequently to keep Annette's memory alive for his daughter. While I understood and even agreed with the wisdom of keeping Annette's memory alive, I was beginning to develop an unreasonable jealousy of my predecessor. Elizabeth's rejections combined with Larry's constant reference to Annette's skills and their genetic legacy tended to rub a sore spot on my heart.

"Your mother's smile could light up a room, Elizabeth," Larry loved to say of his former mate. "You have certainly inherited that smile." He took joy in pointing out the blessings of her inherited tumbling skills as well. "That natural ability is one of the reasons Elizabeth has made friends so easily when we moved in the past," Larry explained. "All she had to do was go out in the yard, stand on her head or do a cartwheel, and the kids came running. She got that from Annette." Suddenly it seemed I could do nothing right and Annette had never done anything wrong. I felt I was being compared to an angel.

My failings had seemed even bigger this morning during our argument. Elizabeth's fury had erupted when I said, "I'm sorry, but I have a meeting and won't be home until at least six o'clock. Then I have a chicken that's thawed and must be cooked, which takes an hour. So shopping tonight won't work, but if you clean your room as I have been asking you to do, we'll talk about shopping tomorrow night."

But "no" is something Elizabeth did not tolerate well. "I *have* to get those leos tonight!" she shrieked. "All the good ones will be gone. We don't have time for dinner."

"Well, I'm sorry. I'll be glad to shop for new leotards tomorrow, but only if you have cleaned up that mess in your room," I repeated.

"That's not fair! You can't make me clean my room!" she yelled. And then she hit me with the classic un-bonding phrase, "You're *not* my mother!" followed closely by a flying cereal box. "I hate you!" she screamed as Cocoa Puffs bounced off my back and spilled onto the floor.

"That's fine," I retorted, as my anger now reached the white-hot level. "Since I'm *not* your mother and you hate me, I now have two more reasons why I don't have to take you shopping. And make sure this cereal is picked up when I get home!" I demanded as I left.

For a full twenty minutes, I shook in the car on my way to work. *I know she hates me,* I thought to myself, *and now that makes two of us.*

It was true: I was starting to hate myself for letting my anger get away from me so often. It seemed that since my own mother's death about a year before our wedding, I was more easily provoked to anger than ever before. Yet because it was most frequently aimed at Elizabeth, I was unsure if lingering grief could be blamed as the culprit.

She really pushes my buttons. I can't let her get away with a tantrum every time I say no. These thoughts and the reenactment of our argument played in my head most of the way to work.

"I don't care if she pushes your buttons. These screaming matches between you two have got to stop," Larry would say when he came home from work and learned of our fight. I could imagine the look on Larry's face as he delivered his frequent line, "We've got to have harmony in this house."

Harmony! It seemed to Larry that a verbal declaration of the goal would magically produce his desired result. It was painful for him to watch the two women he loved most in the world constantly at each other's throats. Although we had heard his siren song of harmony on many occasions, our house was anything but harmonious.

So tonight as I entered the house, I was a little wary, wondering what Elizabeth's demeanor would be after our scuffle this morning. I headed to the closet to change clothes before taking Pandy on our walk; however, the tranquility I usually found by gazing out our living room window as I passed came to an abrupt halt. My eyes fell on the wall next to the front door, and I stared in disbelief. There in the wall of our beautiful entryway was a gaping hole—a hole the exact size of the front doorknob. "Elizabeth!" I shrieked.

It was clear to me that Miss Elizabeth had expressed her anger by slamming the door into the wall. Just as Pandy and I were about to form a posse to bring the guilty to justice, Larry pulled into the driveway. I greeted him at the door with my "You won't believe what she's done now" expression.

"Hi, how's my sweetheart?" he asked in a pleasant tone, ignoring my facial expression. He quickly offered a kiss.

I offered my cheek. "Your sweetheart is in a snit. Come look at this!"

Larry entered the living room and stopped dead in his tracks upon seeing the wall. "Whoa, what happened here?"

I proposed the only plausible explanation and recounted my morning argument with Elizabeth. "She did this to spite me," I proclaimed. "She was furious that I wouldn't go shopping, so after I left for work, she probably slammed the door into the wall on her way out to catch the school bus."

Just then Elizabeth bounced through the front door and into Larry's open arms.

"Hi, Daddy. Come see the picture I made for you at school today." she said, squeezing him with a tight hug.

"I'd love to see the picture, honey, but first, do you know how this hole got in the wall here?" he asked, pointing to the mini-crater.

"Well, maybe when I opened the door, the wind caught it or something and it hit the wall on accident. I'm not sure. I don't really know," Elizabeth said with a straight face.

I rolled my eyes and thought, *That's ridiculous. It would take a force-five tornado blowing through this room to shove that doorknob through a wall and leave a hole that big.*

"So you think it might have happened by accident when you opened the door?" Larry repeated. *I can't believe he's buying a word of this nonsense. He wasn't here this morning when Cocoa Puffs were flying.* I seethed in silence.

"Uh-huh," Elizabeth mumbled. She seemed to consider the matter closed and started up the stairs to get the drawing she had made. Finally I could take no more. "Young lady, you know very well what happened here. You were mad at me this morning over the leotards, and when I left, your anger got out of control, and you slammed the door into the wall intentionally. Now admit it!"

She sat wide-eyed on the stairs and looked at me in stunned amazement. No one had *ever* launched such accusatory, tough talk at Elizabeth before.

Really! What is she thinking? I'll show her that I can always get my way with my dad. My sweet-and-innocent-daughter routine never fails to win his heart over. All I have to do is show him my drawing and tell him I made it especially for him. This dumb hole-in-the-wall thing will blow right over. I will win!

"Now hold on, Kali. How do you know she did this?" Larry growled. "Let's sort out the facts before we start accusing anybody. Maybe one of us did it without realizing it, or maybe it was the house-keeper when she came to clean last week."

Does he really believe what he's saying? I wondered. *There is absolutely no chance I wouldn't have noticed that hole for five days.* I was so stunned by this development that I couldn't believe my own ears, but I angrily kept after Elizabeth, hoping she would break down and confess.

All at once, in the midst of my lecture on being more careful with cereal boxes and doors on windy days, Elizabeth began to giggle. I sensed some motion behind me and turned to see Larry doing a flaw-less Chevy Chase impersonation. He was making faces behind my back and mimicking me! I felt as if I were in *The Twilight Zone* or maybe *Candid Camera*. This couldn't be happening! But Elizabeth thought it was hilarious.

Eventually I learned that Larry wasn't really trying to hurt me and that humor was an effective tool with Elizabeth—in fact, one of the few things Larry knew would work. What seemed to me like an intentional insult was merely an attempt by a laid-back daddy to dif-fuse a volatile situation. He knew Elizabeth would laugh if he played off my overly dramatic style. Their shared humor frequently united them and was one of the ways Larry had maintained his sanity as an overwhelmed single parent. Not only did I fail to comprehend all this, I took it personally. I was embarrassed and so hurt that I couldn't even speak.

Larry tried to put an end to the incident. "She said she didn't do it, and if she did, it was an accident. Let's get over it. It's just a wall; I can fix it."

Well, we may be able to repair the wall, I thought, *but my authority in Elizabeth's eyes has suffered irreparable damage.*

Attempting damage control, Larry suggested that Elizabeth be more careful in the future, but I felt like any hopes I ever had of being an authority figure to Elizabeth were now gone. To me this was much more than a simple drywall project; it was an undermining of the authentic parenting role I hoped to have in this family. I had gambled on the "more mom, less friend" approach and lost.

Larry was more concerned with the effect my heavy-handed crackdown was having on a sensitive little girl, and in hindsight I see that had I used a little more humor and a few kid gloves, my issues with Elizabeth might not have placed Larry in the referee role so often.

Deep inside my heart was a caring mother trying to teach her child about anger management. Somehow, though, I overlooked my own anger and the fact that I too had lost my temper in the midst of the argument. I had allowed my frustration to pile up, and the hole-in-the-wall incident was a strong indication that I was impaired when it came to expressing myself with Elizabeth. In her mind, I was an unreasonable, blaming shrew (and a powerless one at that). Not only was the battle over but I had lost the war! Sure, skirmishes would arise from time to time, but we both knew who had the nuclear weapons.

To make matters worse, Larry would be leaving on Monday for a business trip, and I would be "home alone." The entire wall incident had established two facts in my mind: Elizabeth could skillfully turn her dad's focus from what she had done to how badly I had overreacted, and she was now fully aware that while she was armed to the teeth, I barely wielded a cap pistol in Larry's eyes. I was terrified of how she might use that knowledge.

The morning Larry left town, I kissed him goodbye with great trepidation, for I would be in supposed charge of his precious daughter for an entire week!

"You two sweethearts be good while I'm gone," Larry called out. Elizabeth ran to his arms for one last hug. She watched out the window, tears welling up in her eyes as he pulled out of the driveway.

At least before Dad got married, I could stay with Amanda when he went away on business. This is going to be awful. I've got to stay here alone with Monster Mom. Uh-oh—I forgot to ask Dad for lunch money before he left. I hate having to ask Kali for anything, but I really don't have a choice.

Elizabeth came into my office and sweetly asked, "Kali, can I please have some lunch money?" My anxiety melted a little upon seeing her soft demeanor. "Of course. How much do you need?" I asked, reaching for my purse. I was totally clueless about the price of a school lunch, but I was certain the day was long gone when a kid could get two chocolate chip cookies for a nickel. "Will five dollars be enough?"

"Yes. Thank you," Elizabeth said.

That wasn't as hard as I thought it would be.

She's probably just as uneasy about this as I am. I struggled for something to say that would ease the tension for both of us. As if inspired from above, I remembered that Elizabeth and I had two very important things in common—we both had lost our mothers, and we missed them very much. I went with my instincts.

"Elizabeth, I was just thinking. We are very much alike in a way," I started out hesitantly. She looked at me wide-eyed and questioning.

Searching for some common ground, I pressed on: "We both have lost our mothers."

I watched her eyes as the idea bounced about in her head. "Yeah," she said, "but it's not the same. You said goodbye to your mother and I never did."

Whoa—this was news! I thought I was familiar with every detail surrounding her mother's death, since Larry had relayed the story to me with agonizing frequency.

Larry and Annette had recently relocated to Austin. They hadn't been in town long enough to make many friends, so instead of hosting their annual Super Bowl party, they took in an early-afternoon college basketball game and then headed to Luby's for a quick bite to eat. After the meal, little Elizabeth said, "Mommy, I gotta go potty." Annette excused herself, took Elizabeth by the hand, and escorted her to the ladies' room while Larry waited alone at the table.

Moments later, two young girls came running out of the bathroom toward Larry, crying out with panicked voices, "Your wife is passed out in the bathroom!"

The chaos that followed would torment Larry for years to come. When he burst into the restroom, he found Annette unconscious and slumped down by the sink, where she had apparently been washing her hands. He yanked open the bathroom door and yelled, "Somebody call 911!"

In a flurry of activity, the ambulance arrived and Annette was placed inside. Larry desperately wanted to stay by her side, and a kindly restaurant patron offered to bring Elizabeth to the hospital so Larry could ride in the ambulance.

When Elizabeth arrived at the hospital, a gentle nurse led her to the private waiting room where she reunited with her dad. Soon the nurse came back and invited Elizabeth to come and play while Larry anxiously awaited the doctor's report. It did not take long.

At 4:13 PM, approximately the same moment in 1985 that most

of the country was watching Joe Montana march his 49ers teammates to Super Bowl victory, an emergency room doctor in Texas was delivering devastating news with long-reaching consequences: "I'm sorry, Mr. Schnieders. She's gone."

Annette Laaser Schnieders was only thirty-three years old and five months pregnant with a baby girl. The cause of death was officially pronounced: mitral valve prolapse syndrome. Doc Laaser later struggled to offer a medical explanation to a shocked son-in-law desperate for answers. "Syndrome," Doc said simply and tenderly, "is another word for 'God only knows.'"

Remembering the story in my mind and imagining the wounds our subject was reopening in Elizabeth's heart, I calculated the risk of my next question and then proceeded with caution: "Honey, what do you remember about that day?"

"I just remember being confused when Mommy fell on the bathroom floor, and then later at the hospital when I saw my dad looking so sad, I wanted to make him feel better. But mostly I remember the nurses in the hospital were being really nice to me. One even brought me a teddy bear and some toys to play with while Dad went to say goodbye to Mommy. That's when I made my big mistake."

"Mistake? Honey, you were only three years old. What mistake could you possibly have made?" I asked.

"Well, one of the nurses asked me if I wanted to go tell Mommy goodbye or if I would rather go get a Coke." She paused, looked away, and then continued, "I took the Coke."

I was stunned by the weight of such immense guilt on such small shoulders and wounded by the look of remorse in Elizabeth's eyes. I started to understand how a loving father like Larry could be so compassionate toward his daughter's grief that he'd vow *nothing* would ever hurt her again. With the pain of Elizabeth's confession ringing in my ears, I came as close as I would ever come to comprehending Larry's overprotective behavior and his parental quest to prevent even the tiniest tear from staining her rosy cheeks—even to her detriment.

I realized it was not a matter of refusing to correct her; he simply could not bear to see her cry, because he equated tears with hurting her. He could not yet see the *loving* side of discipline.

Is it possible that this is why I am in her life? I mused. *To be a voice of reason that requires respect and points out unacceptable conduct, even though my attempts at discipline are not upheld? Maybe this child truly needs a friend who will help provide balance in her world—balance that tells her the truth in love and avoids loving blindly in spite of the truth.*

I think this middle-of-the-road straddle thing is what makes a stepparent's job so difficult. For birth mothers, the lines are not blurred, because teaching manners and implementing discipline is part of the job description. But stepparents usually need to start with a friendship posture and wait to be invited into a more authoritative role. Most of us who venture into stepparenthood long to know that our decisions will not be second-guessed, our consequences reversed, or our boundaries ignored. And certainly the best way to avoid confusion and frustration is to obtain agreement on our limitations in advance.

Obviously, I'd already blown this one.

Yet as ignorant as I was on the subject of being a stepmom, hearing this heart-wrenching story from Elizabeth's own lips awakened the best thing I had going for me: I was a woman and therefore I knew how to comfort. I reached out tenderly to hug her.

Unfortunately, Elizabeth was not yet ready to accept comfort from me, and she instantly pulled away. I took a deep breath and tried to keep the huge lump in my throat from choking the words I struggled to form. Elizabeth had been carrying this burden all these years, but at least now I had heaven-sent insight into the deep source of her anger. I took some solace in knowing that this was not all about me as I had imagined.

"Honey, you were only a baby. You didn't even understand what was happening. You must not blame yourself. Any child would say yes to a Coke," I said in my most soothing tone.

How can she even compare losing her mom to me losing mine? I mean, she's a grown-up. It's normal for adults to lose people when they get old. Why, Kali's mother must have been at least sixty! She's right about one thing though: I was only a baby. Sometimes I still feel like a baby—a baby that needs her real mother. It's not fair!

"Well, maybe *you* don't think it was a mistake, but *I* do. Anyway, I've got to catch the bus," Elizabeth said, running for the door. "I can't be late for school."

Our tender, revealing moment was brief and fleeting. But it *had* happened.

I brushed my tears away and promised myself I would be more patient and less judgmental of her in the future. Perhaps if Elizabeth's guilt could be released, her angry little heart could heal. Eventually this frightened child might become willing to risk loving another mother. I wanted to follow where God was leading us, but doing so wasn't going to be easy. We would have to take it one day at a time. I thought about Paul's words: "Let us not become weary in doing good, for at the proper time we will reap a harvest if we do not give up" (Galatians 6:9, NIV). Not giving up—that was going to be the challenge.

If Only I Had Known . . .
- The natural parent's opinions always rule regarding the child.
- It's better to tiptoe into discipline after establishing friendship. *Connect* before you *correct*.
- Tantrums might not mean a spoiled child; they may reveal unresolved grief.

What I Would Have Done Differently
While trying to blend two parenting styles, I'm afraid I was using the Cuisinart method rather than gently folding myself into the family. Although it was not in my nature, things probably would have been more peaceful had I kept better control of my own anger and not reacted so strongly to Elizabeth's behavior. It would have been difficult not to take her actions personally, yet if I'd been able to accomplish this at least some of the time, I might have grown to understand her sooner.

When I voiced my frustrations to Larry, he didn't hear my observations as love; rather, he took them as personal criticisms. So I felt rejected, discouraged, and confused. Perhaps I could have held back my complaints early in the marriage, giving us some time to meld as a family. It would have allowed Larry and Elizabeth to see my love and commitment before they saw my determination to change them.

Reflecting on Your Own Family
- What negative behaviors have you seen in your stepchildren that might have been motivated by grief and pain rather than by a simple case of lack of discipline?
- When have you strongly disagreed with your husband about a parenting issue, and how did you handle it?
- Do you feel the right approach for a stepparent is to be a friend first? Why or why not?

- How can you know what level of discipline your family will accept from you, and what are some things you can do to increase your disciplinary effectiveness?

❋ Chapter Four ❋

Stepping into Cinderella's Slippers

Spoil your husband, but don't spoil your children—that's my philosophy.
—Louise Sevier Giddings Currey,
on being chosen Mother of the Year

"Well, she's no June Cleaver, that's for sure!" Elizabeth lamented to her friend Amanda. "Kali's more like Judge Judy." I was working in the office next to Elizabeth's room and could easily overhear the girls' animated conversation. When I heard my name, my ears perked up. *They must think I can't hear through the wall,* I thought.

Elizabeth was eager for a sympathetic ear, so she rapidly poured out the details of her disillusionment with family life since our wedding. "So much for my hopes of mother-daughter shopping sprees and weekends filled with dress-up tea parties," she began. "The only one who dresses up around here is Kali! She plays dress-up all the time. The minute I see Kali pulling her formal out of the closet, I know that the wicked stepmother is off to another ball with my dad and that I get to be Cinderella—left at home with a sitter again!"

55

"Ouch," I said under my breath. Elizabeth's words stung because they were partially true. Larry's career in public relations involved frequent entertaining, many late evenings, and formal galas. Elizabeth's comment brought to mind the Governor's Inaugural Ball and how the evening must have seemed to her. Larry was dressed in his tux and I in a chiffon evening dress. We whirled off for an evening of fine dining, dancing, and schmoozing with interesting people while Elizabeth stayed behind with her older cousin and a frozen pizza.

The scenario was not uncommon. Nevertheless, we felt blessed to have cousin Kelly, an architectural student, living nearby in Lawrence. And until now, my guilt in leaving Elizabeth at home had been lessened by Larry's rationale: "It's an excellent opportunity for some extended-family bonding."

I heard Amanda gasp. "You mean she actually goes to fancy balls and expects you to clean the house and stuff?" she asked in astonishment. "Wow, I thought *my* stepmother was a witch!"

"Oh, that's not the worst of it, Amanda," Elizabeth continued dramatically, sensing the empathy oozing forth from her best friend (and failing to mention that household chores were to her a foreign concept). "When they aren't going to a ball, they're on the golf course. Can you believe they've played that stupid game nearly every weekend since the honeymoon?"

Hey, I've got permanent bleacher bruises from watching Elizabeth perform in gymnastics on most of those weekends. I fought my impulse to rush in and set the record straight. This was an opportunity to see how she portrayed me to her friends.

"And get this," Elizabeth said, pausing for dramatic effect. "Sometimes they go off to play golf and leave me in this scary house all by myself!"

"Man, I think that'd be cool," said Amanda. "You could do anything you wanted after they left."

"Yeah, that's what I thought at first, but after watching about a million cartoons, I got so bored that I took all the cushions off the sofa and piled them up a mile high like they do with the mats at the gym. I jumped off the kitchen counter and did a flip onto the cushions, but they slipped and I nearly split my head open. Of course, I never could say anything about it 'cause I'm not supposed to practice tumbling if no one's home, but I figured it would serve them right if I killed myself while they played golf."

"Wow!" Amanda cried out.

Now *I* was the one who gasped. *That is dangerous! I'd better let Larry know about this.* It was true that golf had been popping up on our calendar whenever we had no gymnastics commitments. Elizabeth never had mentioned feeling scared before, and having grown up a latchkey kid myself, I saw no reason to object when Larry proposed an occasional golf outing. We both felt we were leaving Elizabeth in a safe environment. Ours was a community with a Neighborhood Watch system, and we were on a first-name basis with most of our neighbors. Therefore, we felt our precautions of setting the alarm system and carrying our cell phone in the golf cart had reassured Elizabeth sufficiently. She knew we were within easy reach with our front door only five minutes from the golf course. Given Elizabeth's flair for the dramatic, I also wondered how much of this was actual anxiety and how much was embellished for Amanda's benefit.

Larry was a vigilant, protective dad, and because he never questioned Elizabeth's safety, I always rested peacefully in his assurance. Our golf outings had the added benefit of fanning the flames of romance between us because while on the course, we experienced the harmony that was missing around the house. These mini-excursions enabled me to cope better when we returned home.

Most important, our golfing did a world of good for my husband. He desperately needed a fun, physical stress outlet. When the tragedy of Annette's death had thrust him into a solo-parenting role, he didn't have time for sports or any of the normal adult leisure activities.

"I remember sitting in my parents' den after the funeral, reeling from shock and sickened by grief," Larry explained one day, recounting the events immediately following Annette's death. "I was telling my dad how much I dreaded a future without Annette. As I sat wondering how I would ever be able to raise Elizabeth while juggling my all-consuming career, I watched her play on the floor with her doll. *My little angel,* I thought.

"Suddenly, as if cued by a Hollywood script, a broad ray of sunlight came streaming through the nearby window. A beam illuminated Elizabeth's face with such tender beauty. The sun's rays seemed almost like God's fingers caressing her cheeks and wiping away her sorrow. Those heavenly sunbeams were also a reminder that Annette—whose nickname from childhood had been 'Sunshine'—would always be with us. While I didn't hear God's voice, the message was clear enough: I *had* to snap out of this paralyzing blue funk in honor of Annette and for Elizabeth's sake. I was all my daughter had left. Caring for her needs would not only be my life's goal, it would be my salvation from a despairing pit of grief."

From that day forward, Larry immersed himself in Elizabeth. Mercifully, the outpouring of compassion from friends and family and the heartwarming support at work not only eased his pain but also bolstered Larry's spirit and breathed fresh life into his corporate commitment.

Nevertheless, Mr. Mom was hopping between parent-teacher conferences and work meetings. He juggled briefcases, lunch boxes, and backpacks, still managing to keep pace with the best mom in the carpool. For five years, Larry had dressed and coiffured Elizabeth like a pro, never missing a step in dancing to the beat of the company drum. The two-ended candle burning was taking a toll, and with me on the scene, Super Dad finally saw an opportunity to take some time for himself. After building a house on the golf course for his new bride, Larry decided the time had come to satisfy some of his own needs.

Between Larry's need for tee times and Elizabeth's desire for tea parties, I didn't know which way to turn to stay in everyone's good graces and out of their doghouse. Larry's solution had been simple: we would make golf our "family sport."

Larry was wise enough to know that good marriages and happy families take effort. (And making me a golf widow would not have been a step in the right direction.) In an attempt to get those golf carts rolling, he soon located a miniature set of clubs for Elizabeth and presented me with my first Mother's Day gift: a golf outfit, clubs, shoes, gloves—the whole shebang. The pastel golf balls cinched the deal.

"Oooh, I love these robin-egg blue ones!" I exclaimed, rolling the little beauty between my gloved fingers.

Larry had generously provided everything a woman could possibly need for the sport of golf except the one thing I'd needed most: athletic ability. Nevertheless, I had waited fifteen years for the man of my dreams, and I was not about to let him run off without me for five hours at a stretch on the weekends. And Elizabeth wasn't about to have me running off alone with her dad! So we all piled into a golf cart and headed for the first tee box. Coach Larry was very patient with his pro-golf prodigies, but our outing was headed for the rough from the start.

"Elizabeth, you are a natural," her proud papa proclaimed. "With that swing and some practice, you could become a female Tiger Woods!"

"I don't want to be Tiger Woods; I want to be Mary Lou Retton," Elizabeth retorted. "Golf is a boring, stupid game. I'm already sick of it. I want to go home!"

"Honey, you don't have to play if you don't want to. How about driving the cart awhile?" I coaxed, hoping to avoid a rift. "Very few ten-year-olds get to drive."

Elizabeth glared at me but slid behind the wheel and floored the gas pedal. Being stuck in the middle, I quickly wearied of our junior driver's attitude. Elizabeth apparently felt that being chauffeur meant she was entitled to half of the seat, so she squeezed us into the other half.

Why do we all have to cram into this stupid cart, and why do I have to sit by her? This has to change. My dad never played this boring game all the time until Kali came along. What do I have to do to make her just go away?

"Elizabeth, *please* scoot over just a little bit," I implored. My irritation was increasing faster than my golf score, but every request for consideration seemed to evoke an elbow to my ribs.

"Gross!" Elizabeth complained in disgust. "Dad, how am I supposed to drive with Kali's sweaty thighs touching me? Move over, Kali!" She stomped hard on my foot.

"Ouch!" I yelped. "That hurt!" I eyeballed Larry, waiting for him to jump to my defense.

"You're overreacting again, Kali," Larry said. "It couldn't have hurt that much. Besides, she didn't do it on purpose. Here—just move closer to me."

Obviously, the stress of the situation brought out the worst in all of us, as is so common in stepfamilies. Looking back, I can see now how childish our behavior had become—not just Elizabeth's, but mine and Larry's too. At the time, we seemed unable to rise above it all.

Elizabeth gave me her "See I always win" look when Larry was occupied with his backswing. As Larry climbed back into the cart, Elizabeth quickly accelerated before he could get safely seated. "Hey, slow down there!" Larry warned, but Elizabeth ignored his remark and accelerated all the more. "Elizabeth, I mean it—this is not safe. If you don't slow down, I won't let you drive anymore."

And so it went for about three outings until finally Elizabeth refused to golf with us at all. Verbally I protested, but secretly I was pleased. I longed to have a peaceful day with my sweetheart without the child spoiling our time together.

Maybe if I refuse to go, they'll stop playing golf so much and we'll do something fun for a change.

So we began enjoying some much-needed couple time on the golf course on weekends. At home Elizabeth usually was occupied with her favorite television programs or playing with friends. I never realized how lonely she was or that she felt left out. I just knew how much she hated being around me, so I rationalized that she was glad whenever I wasn't around. Unfortunately, now that I had become Larry's golf playmate, Elizabeth saw me as even more of a rival. With both of us having such competitive natures, it was *not* a healthy situation.

We spent so much time immersed in gymnastics that golf was just the oasis of romance we both needed. The frequency of our tee times increased, and I finally took some golf lessons and tried to get the hang of it. As long as Elizabeth wasn't there to engage me in battle, Larry and I got along so well that my loving feelings toward him regularly resurfaced.

Nevertheless, the golfing habit was becoming so frequent that I began to feel guilty about leaving Elizabeth at home. I voiced my apprehension, but Larry was unconcerned. "We'll stop by the house and check on her when we get to the seventh hole. Maybe she'll change her mind and join us for the back nine," he would usually say.

Now as I look back on this experience, I have to say that if I was ever offered an opportunity to pick one thing for a "do-over," this would definitely be what I would choose. Among all of the bone-headed decisions I have made as a stepmother, my decision not to seek one-on-one time with Elizabeth early in the marriage was my gravest error. In retrospect, I should have put my foot down and said, "Larry, you can play golf all weekend if you must, but I'm going to spend some time with Elizabeth." I could have taken her shopping, out to lunch, or to the movies—anything she'd enjoy that we could do together.

That one simple decision could have changed the entire course of our relationship, but alas, I wimped out. I attached myself to my husband like a Siamese twin and took what seemed like the easy path. By playing golf, I hoped to avoid arguments, frazzled nerves, and bruised shins—and keep my marriage vital.

I mulled over the desire Elizabeth had mentioned to Amanda for girly shopping trips and tea parties with me. The few times we had ventured out together usually resulted in a fight, and the only tea parties I could imagine with her involved a nine-year-old lacing my orange pekoe with arsenic. I discounted her comment and contented myself with what I considered to be the facts. Fact one: She could be mean as a snake. Fact two: She really wanted nothing to do with me.

So listening to Elizabeth and Amanda's conversation was giving me even more food for thought. Could it be that Elizabeth would have rather spent some time with me than stay home alone?

I really want to do girly things like my friends do with their moms. I guess Kali would be better than nothing. At least I'd know she cared about me, and it would sure beat staying here all alone while they play golf all the time.

I heard Amanda sigh as she processed all that Elizabeth had shared with her. "Man, am I glad my dad isn't as into golf as yours is," Amanda said in a melancholy tone. "Still, I have to deal with stuff that you never have to worry about. My folks may be divorced, but they still fight as though they were married. You wouldn't believe how confused I get living in two different homes with two sets of rules."

"What kind of rules?" Elizabeth asked.

"Well, at Mom's house I have to go to bed by ten *every* night, but when I stay at Dad's, I don't even have a bedtime. Then Mom makes me eat those yucky green and white vegetables that look like brains and trees; Dad lets me eat whatever I want. Of course, my stepmom thinks I should have to help with the dishes, but my mom likes to do them herself. You should try keeping *that* straight. The good part is that they both feel guilty about the divorce, so I get some pretty cool stuff if I play my cards right."

"Well, I can tell you a few things about rules," Elizabeth interrupted. "They made me see a shrink! His office was creepy, and I had to talk to this weird doctor who asked me why I hate Kali so much, as if that's not obvious. It was just like you see in the movies—that boring old man just sat there and stared at me. By the time I got home, all I wanted to do was take a nap. Anyway, Dr. Fancy-Pants said we needed some house rules, so Dad and Kali came home and made up a whole binder full of junk I'm not allowed to do."

"You mean they actually wrote the rules down?" Amanda asked incredulously.

"That's only half of it! They made me sign an agreement not to do that stuff, and every time I break a rule, they pull that big binder out and take away a privilege. The rules are really dumb, like "no eye rolling" and "no sassing." I'm sure we never had any stupid rulebook when Mommy was alive. All this is Kali's fault. See why I hate her?"

Their chatter hushed for a moment, and I could visualize the girls lamenting their hellish home lives. As I sat contemplating Elizabeth's words, I didn't know whether to laugh or to cry.

I remembered the night Elizabeth's third-grade teacher, Miss Stone, recommended we consider some psychological counseling. I was so embarrassed during the parent-teacher conference as I listened to her concerns.

"I don't want to alarm you," Miss Stone began gently, "but Elizabeth seems to have stored up a lot of anger about your marriage. You can see that it is particularly directed at Kali in this typical example from her journal. When I read Elizabeth's thoughts, I felt I should share with you some comments that particularly bothered me."

Miss Stone pointed to a section called "My So-Called Mom." Elizabeth described a detailed plot to do me in by putting poisonous snakes in my bed. "Yikes!" I gasped upon reading the words. "Elizabeth was certainly letting her thoughts and feelings fly freely."

"Yes, I'm aware Elizabeth has some issues with Kali," Larry explained, "but I don't think there's any real danger here." It was difficult for him to believe that Elizabeth would actually do me harm. "This is just a child letting off steam," he said simply.

Miss Stone agreed. "Oh, I'm sure she would never carry out any of these plans," she said, "but it does indicate that she's struggling and might benefit from a psychological evaluation. Elizabeth's been through a lot in her young life, and this is a sign that she may not be coping very well. I'd simply feel a lot better knowing that a professional was involved."

I had known there was something beneath Elizabeth's behavior, but I hadn't been able to convince Larry that counseling was necessary or beneficial. Whenever I'd broached the subject, he would remind me of all the positives. "Look at her grades, for Pete's sake. She's a perfectly happy child. She's smiling all the time, she's outgoing with her friends—those aren't signs of deep-seated problems. I know more about Elizabeth than anyone does, and I don't think counseling is necessary."

Larry was right: he *did* know Elizabeth better than anybody else did. It's also true that sometimes an outsider (particularly a stepparent who truly cares about the child's well-being) can see storm clouds looming on the horizon that a natural parent might interpret as nothing more than a gentle spring rain. It's risky business for a stepmom to try to herd the family into the storm shelter when Dad has decided that an umbrella will do the trick. The stepmom's concern can be misinterpreted and her motives called into question. Then the phrase "evil stepmother" comes to mind.

But finally I had an ally. Alarmed by the sincerity of Miss Stone's concerns, the closed subject was now on the discussion table again with Larry. He soon made a counseling appointment with Dr. Yancy, a nearby psychologist.

When the day for our appointment arrived, I was relieved. I had high hopes that Elizabeth would finally receive the help she needed to work through her anger and lingering grief over her mother's death as well as my presence in her life. I was certain Dr. Yancy would recommend extended counseling sessions to help us negotiate an agreement about what constituted acceptable behavior in our home.

I was stunned when the doctor simply said, "Well, Elizabeth does have some trust issues with Kali, and she is worried that you two might have another child. Beyond that, you are basically dealing with the spoiled-child syndrome. I recommend you set down some rules."

That's it? I screamed silently to myself. *Spoiled-child syndrome? Trust issues? I could have diagnosed that myself.*

I brought up the possibility of some additional visits to monitor our progress. I envisioned future sessions where we would discuss how well the "rules" were being followed and enforced. I hoped Dr. Yancy would offer impartial opinions that would help me to have more compassion for Larry's position and enable Larry to see that some of my parental instincts were on target. I felt that all three of us needed a better understanding of each other.

"Oh, I don't think that will be necessary, Mrs. Schnieders. If you just make a few rules and enforce them consistently, that should correct things," Dr. Yancy concluded.

Lord, you know how hard I've tried and how long I've waited to get this child some counseling! I prayed silently. *Larry will be even more firmly convinced that none is needed, thanks to Dr. Yancy. I know Elizabeth needs professional help to work through her anger. I'm not trained for that! I feel as though I'm trying to claw my way out of quicksand, but with every move, I'm sinking further down.*

My thoughts advanced from prayer to betrayal to homicide. Now *I* was contemplating poisonous snakes in someone's bed (a certain doctor's bed, to be specific). I left his office only having gained one consoling thought from the experience: *Well, at least we'll have some rules to go by around the house.*

Unfortunately, *I* was usually the one running for the rulebook. Now that I knew how much Elizabeth hated that book, I was perplexed about what to do next.

After Amanda left, I decided to make another stab at friendship with Elizabeth. The next time I saw her slipping on her Rollerblades, I asked if I could tag along. She always seemed less reluctant to being friendly toward me if Larry wasn't around.

"Sure, let's go!" she said enthusiastically.

Our skating adventure began well: I strolled, Elizabeth rolled, and we chatted merrily holding hands. We discussed school and the new girl she'd met. "I'm hoping that because she's new too, maybe we can be friends," Elizabeth confided. I was always sympathetic to her need for new friends, and I hoped she would soon find someone to take Amanda's place as confidante.

I enjoyed watching Elizabeth sail along, bounding over small obstacles in the sidewalk.

"Wheeee!" she squealed with delight, landing perfectly after a gentle leap. As we neared the end of our street, I glanced down the long cement tunnel that branched off from the sidewalk. I could see the sloping curve that continued down a steep hill. Actually, the tunnel was part of the golf-cart path and was never intended to be a skating ramp.

Wow! Look at that cool tunnel. I've never skated down a hill this big before. What a perfect chance to impress Kali. She'll be so blown away. Now she'll see that I'm a great kid and fun to be around.

What happened next remains a mental and emotional blur. All I know with certainty is that Elizabeth's skates made a beeline for that tunnel and her hand slipped from my grasp. The whole scene felt like a horrifying, slow-motion nightmare. We both screamed, and I ran for all I was worth. I tried in vain to grab her back to safety, but she was swept down the tunnel like a little twig caught in a flash flood. Then I heard her shriek as she landed in a heap.

I'll never forget the look of betrayal that flashed across Elizabeth's face.

"Why did you let go of me?" she screamed. "I'm bleeeeeeeeeeding!"

I could see nasty scrapes on her knees and elbows. "Honey, I am *so* sorry. I had no idea you were going to go down that tunnel, and before I knew what was happening, you were gone."

I can't believe Kali didn't even try to catch me. She probably let go on purpose. I could have hit my head and died for all she cares. This cut will probably leave a scar for the rest of my life—like I really needed a reminder of how much she hates me.

If Elizabeth had trust issues with me before, this incident was certainly no help. No explanation would convince her that it was all an innocent accident. Completely lost in all the fuss was the fact that I'd initiated joining her on the skating expedition in the first place.

The next day, we called Elizabeth from the eighteenth hole to tell her we had finished our round and would pick her up and go out for Chinese food.

"That won't be necessary," she said. "I have a surprise. I cooked dinner for you myself!"

When we walked in the door, I couldn't believe my eyes. Elizabeth was dressed in the lovely emerald dress she had worn in our wedding. I was amazed by how well it fit, as it had been more than a year since the day she goose-stepped down the aisle. She led us out into the backyard, where she had set an elaborate table with candles and cloth napkins. The scene was perfectly adorable.

We sat down to two salad bowls filled with cabbage (that she had mistaken for lettuce) and two frozen dinners removed from their plastic trays and nestled on china dinner plates. She even had a "chocolate mousse" for our dessert (chocolate pudding scraped out of Jell-o pudding cups and scooped into stemmed glasses).

"And now for the entertainment!" she announced.

She darted into the house and returned with her clarinet. Elizabeth had not taken many lessons, but she serenaded us there on the lawn with as much heart as a professional musician from the finest philharmonic orchestra. Meanwhile, Larry and I choked down cabbage and lukewarm noodles while "oooing" and "ahhhhing" as though we were dining on a meal fit for royalty.

Later that night after Elizabeth was tucked into bed, I went to finish the dinner dishes. I lovingly dried the crystal goblets, and grateful tears appeared as I pondered the elaborate dinner gift I'd received that night. I smiled and wondered if perhaps Elizabeth had forgiven me for the skating episode after all.

As I put the last goblet in the cabinet, a gentle breeze blew through the open kitchen window and kissed my cheek. It seemed to whisper as it passed, "Tonight's meal was more than dinner; it was a cabbage-flavored olive branch of peace."

Many years later, I learned that the dinner was even more than an olive branch; it was Elizabeth's way of getting our attention. She wanted us to see that she missed us when we played golf and that she wanted us to spend more time with her.

But Elizabeth didn't have the words to express all this, and Larry and I didn't have the eyes to see it. Would the next few years have been different if we'd recognized the truth? Probably. We'll never know.

At least I saw the potential for peace in Elizabeth's loving gesture. And in time, I came to see that peace with Elizabeth was a come-and-go thing. I learned to be grateful each time harmony appeared between us — for whatever reason and however briefly.

> *The dove came to him toward evening, and behold,*
> *in her beak was a freshly picked olive leaf.*
> —GENESIS 8:11

If Only I Had Known . . .

- No matter what they say, children want time with their parents—stepparents included.
- "Family activities" only count if the kids actually enjoy them.
- Peace doesn't come easily in any stepfamily.

What I Would Have Done Differently

Family activities are wonderful, but deep and abiding relationships must be built one-on-one over a period of time. If I'd pursued Elizabeth with the same intensity I'd lavished on Larry, good things probably would have happened. I wish I'd been able to rise above my fear of "yet another rejection" from Elizabeth and planned weekend outings for the two of us. As much as I loved my time alone with Larry, our marriage probably would have improved just as much if Elizabeth and I had felt more harmony between us.

Reflecting on Your Own Family

- How much time do you spend with your stepchildren doing things together that they enjoy?
- Have you noticed anything in particular that any of your stepchildren have done that might have been a genuine cry for attention?
- What are some concrete actions you could take to improve the peace and bonding between you and your stepchildren?

* Chapter Five *

One Step Forward, Two Steps Back

Marriage is our last, best chance to grow up.
—JOSEPH BARTH

Larry was leaving on another business trip, but Elizabeth and I had grown accustomed to the drill. His absence no longer terrified us, although I was always slightly apprehensive playing the single-parent role. Each occurrence brought with it a unique mothering opportunity because I never knew if I would be treated to something adorable or deplorable.

I stepped outside to fetch the mail and overheard my daughter cursing out a playmate with gusto and volume: "Ryan, I did *too* sell lemonade to a Royals baseball player. It was George Brett, and he gave me five bucks. You are just a jealous @$%^*&#."

"Elizabeth, get in this house this minute!" I yelled, determined to put a stop to Elizabeth's foul language (which I hoped our neighbors would *not* assume she had learned from me!).

First Kali embarrasses me in front of my friends, and now she doesn't want me to have any! Everyone already knows I have the meanest mother in the universe. She doesn't have to yell at me in front of the whole world just to prove it. I guess I'd better get inside before she yells at me again.

The moment I barked out my parental command, an image from the animated television series *Dinosaurs* flashed through my mind. Daddy Dinosaur, the role model for parental ineffectiveness, often needed to babysit. As soon as Dino-Mom was out of sight, the baby always misbehaved. When Dad attempted to correct his little one, the baby whacked him on the noggin with a huge rattle. With every conk, the baby screamed, "Not the mama, not the mama, not the mama!"

Elizabeth took similar pleasure in smacking me with her version of a verbal "rattle." "You're *not* my mom!" was her favorite declaration.

I mentally put on a helmet and braced myself for the approaching assault. I was astonished when none came. She actually obeyed me and marched herself right home. She then simply looked at me with a strange mixture of emotions that could best be described as sheepish defiance. We both knew this was not appropriate language. For all of our arguing, Larry and I did not have a habit of spewing forth profanity, and I had heard Larry correct Elizabeth's stray words in the past. I figured she'd picked up this "vocabulary" at school. Apparently, she thought it would impress her playmates, not to mention the whole neighborhood!

When she came inside, I told her to sit on the couch, take a time-out, and think about what she'd said. "I'll be back in ten minutes to discuss this," I scolded with as much command as I could muster. Really I was also giving myself a time-out to figure out exactly how to approach the situation and to seek a little divine guidance in the process. *Unless You help me, Lord, I know I'm going to make a mess of this.*

Gosh, she always makes me sit in time-out to think about what I've done. I wonder if she knows that all I can think about is how much she gets on my nerves. Time-out is dumb!

When I returned, Elizabeth was staring out the window with her arms folded tightly across her chest and a scowl on her face. I dreaded the kicking-screaming tantrum that was sure to erupt on the floor the moment I began to speak, and I had no idea what to do if that happened. I decided to take a softer-than-usual approach—sort of woman-to-woman or friend-to-friend. I began by sitting beside her and speaking softly: "Okay, now what was so bad that it required all that filthy talk?"

I sat with my mouth closed and my mind open, determined to give Elizabeth time to explain without interruption. She laid out a tale of "he said, then I said," and I took in every word. When she finished, I summoned my most controlled, gentle tone and explained my point of view. "Elizabeth, I understand that your friends at school may use dirty and disrespectful words, and I doubt that their parents approve either," I began, "but even if every man, woman, and child in Lawrence used the 'f' word and called each other names, it still would not be the right thing to do or the right behavior to copy. To me, it shows either a lack of self-control or a lack of intelligence. I know you are creative enough to think of a more effective way to express your anger, because potty talk will only add more fuel to a fire. Besides, I care too much about you to have other people think you lack intelligence," I concluded, gently patting her leg, "because you're about the smartest girl I know."

I really hate to admit it, but sometimes Kali does have a point. But those bad words just kind of slipped out. She's right about another thing too. I am a smart girl.

Elizabeth's head was leaning against my shoulder now. I hated to have to punish her, but I wanted to be sure the lesson was learned and the behavior not soon repeated. Larry used a very effective technique on occasion, so I followed his example and asked, "What do you think is a reasonable punishment?"

I was often amazed to see Elizabeth's self-punishment to be much more harsh than anything I would have dreamed up, but she didn't offer anything right away, so I presented my own idea: "How about no television tonight?" I asked.

"Oh, but tonight my very favorite show, *Fun House*, is on!" Elizabeth whined.

"Yes, I guess that's what makes it a punishment. It seems to me that unless a little pain is involved, you don't learn the lesson very well."

She grumbled a little, but we agreed to the plan. *That went surprisingly well,* I said to myself as we each went separate directions in the house to ponder what had just occurred. *I don't know where those wise words came from, Lord, but I suspect You had something to do with it.* I was grateful for the Divine Wordsmith, who had undoubtedly blessed my brain with momentary wisdom.

The evening progressed smoothly until it was time for *Fun House*, and then Elizabeth started to get whiny. Apparently, she was making a run at getting me to back down. She was about to learn that my "no" meant no. I heard her mutter something under her breath and picked up enough to know it was a curse word.

Disappointed in light of our earlier chat, I whirled around to confront her. "Elizabeth!" I struggled to practice what I had preached about accelerating fires but took a deep breath and calmed my tone. "I heard what you said. So unless you apologize, I will not be reading any bedtime stories." With that, I left the room.

Later when I was in the bathroom removing my makeup and readying myself for bed, I heard a knock at the door.

"I'm sorry, Kali," came Elizabeth's sincere apology. "Will you please read me a story tonight?"

"I accept your apology, and as soon as I'm finished here, I'll be happy to come up and read you a story. You go pick out a really good one, okay?" I said, my heart now soaring with the joy of a mission accomplished.

As she made her exit, Elizabeth could not resist teasing me by pretending to say a bad word and then changing it at the very end of the last syllable, presumably to demonstrate the creative intelligence I had praised in her earlier.

"You rascal," I teased back, feigning anger. "What am I going to do with you?"

"Why don't you sit down and have another talk with me? That really works!" she said and scampered down the hall.

Wow, that little talk really must have been divinely inspired! I mused as the full impact of our chat took hold. I felt so close to Elizabeth at that moment, and I was keen on reading to her. Skipping the story would have punished me too, because story time got us on the same wavelength; it was often the best part of our day. I was so grateful not to have to miss the magic that night, and I was hoping she might even cuddle fairly close to me as she occasionally did when Larry was out of town (probably because there was no competition over him).

I entered her room, and she had already turned on her mood music. Pachelbel's *Canon in D* was her favorite bedtime song, and I continue to be impressed by the sophistication of her choice. That piece always soothes me and makes me tear up with joy. I was delighted to know that we shared an appreciation for beautiful music.

Elizabeth handed me a book and we settled in together. "*James and the Giant Peach,*" I began with enthusiasm as I read the title. I cherished the moment and silently wished it could always be this way: working through the tough issues and coming together in harmony at day's end.

When I finished the story, we said our "God blesses." When she got around to "God bless Kali," it seemed so heartfelt that I choked up. When it was my turn to talk to God, I think Elizabeth heard the crack in my voice, because she squeezed my hand as I offered my petitions and gratitude: " . . . and thank you for helping us work out our problem earlier and for a daughter that is able to apologize when she is wrong. Help us both to do the right thing when we are tempted to do otherwise. Thank you for bringing Elizabeth into my life. Amen."

I have to admit it's not always so bad having Kali around. I feel kind of weird about it, but tonight I wish she'd even kiss me good night.

I wanted to kiss her cheek, but I'd been rebuffed so many times in the past, I didn't want to press my luck and spoil the tenderness we did share by ending on a sour note. Instead, I took the safe route of patting her little leg.

Though Larry's overnight business trip had initially raised my anxiety level, being alone with Elizabeth had provided some unexpected blessings. With her dad away, Elizabeth could lighten up on her need to prove that I was not in charge. She momentarily seemed to relax into the security of a two-parent family again (as long as she had to deal with only one adult at a time). Perhaps during this brief encounter, she even viewed me as a person—as more than just her dad's wife. I had peeked beneath the veneer of anger and rejection and found a clever girl capable of more than waging wars and escalating battles.

I padded down the steps to my room, fluffed up the pillows, and waited for Larry's nightly long-distance call. As I waited, my mind drifted to the memory of my husband standing between wife and daughter during a bygone fight, saying, "Harmony. How 'bout a little harmony?" *Larry's really on to something with this harmony thing*, I smiled to myself. If only harmony were this easy when the three of us were together.

Unfortunately, when Larry was around, arguments were more frequent in our house. It seemed not only did I clash more with Elizabeth but even arguments between Larry and me cropped up occasionally.

One of the latest had been particularly difficult. And to think it all had begun with such a noble cause.

The Topeka Performing Arts Center (TPAC) was undergoing a major renovation, and because my husband's employer was a sponsor of the project, Larry was heavily involved with the public-relations aspect. It was an exciting opportunity for Larry, and I was very proud of him. However, his workload doubled as the grand opening approached, and I was left with the lion's share of the home duties. I found myself sitting alone at Elizabeth's gymnastics practice with greater frequency. Larry knew that the situation was less than ideal, but for the time being, we simply did what we needed to do.

Even though I was working full-time too, I tried to support Larry by being available for Elizabeth and caring for her needs. We felt the pressures that so many working couples face when both parents are pulled in two directions at once. Slowly I was becoming convinced that one of us in the workforce was plenty. The notion of folding little socks rather than sitting in rush-hour traffic sounded more appealing, and I wondered if more time at home would draw Elizabeth and me closer.

Because financially we could not yet swing it for me to retire from the corporate rat race, I did my best to keep all the plates spinning on their sticks. However, with the increase of Larry's late nights on the Art Center project, I was feeling more like a single parent. As my patience and stamina were fading, Larry brought home a treat guaranteed to put a smile on my face—or so he thought.

"Have I got a nice surprise for you!" he announced as he walked in the front door proudly waving a pair of front-row tickets to the opening-night gala. But before handing me the tickets, he handed me a letter embossed with the TPAC insignia at the top.

The letter started out well enough with a cordial "Dear Mr. Schnieders." Excited to cut to the chase, I read toward the bottom: "Thank you for your contribution to the Topeka Performing Arts Center. In appreciation, you are entitled to a nameplate to be placed on the back of a theater seat. Please indicate how you would like the plaque inscribed."

How thrilling, I thought, sincerely pleased with this special honor. Then my eyes popped out of my head as I read Larry's requested inscription in the space provided: "In memory of Annette Laaser Schnieders." My reaction was very similar to the day my beloved cat strutted in, plopped a dead mouse at my feet, and stepped back, anticipating my joyful admiration. Like the cat, I knew Larry was proud of his accomplishment and his gift to me. But my response was not what he'd hoped it would be.

I was so hurt that I could not even respond. I felt invisible and unappreciated. I guess God must have struck me mute in order to prevent me from screaming out loud all the thoughts that raced through my mind. I handed the letter back to Larry and fled to our bedroom to lick my emotional wounds and be alone with my thoughts. Whenever I am deeply hurt, my initial response is usually to sidestep the issue, which never helps and usually compounds the problem. It takes me awhile, sometimes days, before I can move from anger to tears. I can do "mad" with relative ease, but "sad" is an emotion that initially eludes me, probably when I need it most.

After safely arriving in the bedroom and out of earshot, I fumed and ranted to myself. *Where was Annette while my backside was being tortured by those hard bleachers at the gym? And where was she when I was listening to Elizabeth's frustration after a disappointing gymnastics practice? And for that matter, where was Larry?*

I paced like an injured tigress and allowed my anger to rise into a full head of steam. But the pain was too intense to waste on anger alone; I was uncharacteristically bawling within minutes. Not wanting to be discovered or mollified, I hid in the closet and welcomed the tears as I carried on a one-sided conversation in my mind: *Can you truly be this oblivious to my feelings? All the while, I thought you and I were in this together—in both the home project and the TPAC project.*

But now I see that I was way off. I'm in this project alone, and you are still in it with Annette! First, I have to put up with Elizabeth's favorite anti-bonding phrases: "You're not my mother!" and "You're not the boss of me!" Fine, I can accept that. But I will not accept that I'm not the wife in this marriage. "In sickness and in health" I can handle, but not insignificance! That's asking too much.

Eventually, Larry found my makeshift hideout and tried to calm me down. He patted my hand and said softly, "Kali, I never intended to hurt your feelings" (which, of course, I knew deep down). Nevertheless, given the moment at hand, my husband's pledge of innocence seemed far-fetched.

"Kali, I saw this as only an opportunity to do something nice in Annette's memory, and I figured I'd have a lifetime to do nice things for you. Other than her gravestone, I don't have anything concrete as a memorial to mark her place in my life. I'll put Mr. and Mrs. Larry Schnieders on the plaque if that will make you feel better," he said. But something in his tone left me feeling worse than ever.

Oh, fine, I thought, *now make me feel like a big greedy baby who's trying to grab something for myself at the expense of the dearly departed.* Somehow, whenever we discussed my feelings about Annette, I always came out looking unreasonably jealous. I never had the nerve to ask Larry outright, "Do you feel disloyal to Annette for marrying me? Is this plaque some sort of guilt offering?" I guess I was afraid to hear the answers.

Then the notion struck me like a palm to the forehead: *If Larry feels like an unfaithful husband, maybe Elizabeth has intuitively picked up some of his ambivalence about this marriage. She and I get along much better when Larry's not around. Maybe there's more to our problems than competition for Larry's affection. Maybe there is another loyalty issue at play? Maybe this is why we cannot seem to operate as a harmonious three-some. No wonder I often feel as though I'm living in a game of odd man out. I am the odd woman out!*

I had more questions than answers, but for now the conflict was over. Larry decided the plaque would read, "In memory of Annette Laaser Schnieders, by Larry and Kali Schnieders." It certainly did not feel like victory. I took no comfort and held out no hope that we had reached a new understanding that would forever resolve the Annette issue.

Of course, while it is completely unreasonable to feel competitive with a person who is not even living, every second wife I know has such issues of the heart to reconcile and resolve. Whether the first wife is still in the picture or not, her impact is felt by every member of the family for many years to come. At the time, I could not foresee that a crucial key to conquering the pain that plagued our family would be my acceptance of Annette as a co-mother and ally.

That night, I approached Elizabeth's bedroom and paused outside the door. Larry had just finished reading, and they were moving on to prayers. I could picture the two of them snuggled happily together, an image that warmed my heart and brought tears to my eyes.

Apparently, Elizabeth had grown weary of the traditional "Now I lay me down to sleep . . ." prayer. She protested, "Daddy, I don't really feel like praying. I just say the same things over and over, and some of those words don't make any sense! 'Now I lay-me.' What's a lay-me? And if God really is keeping my soul, when did He take it and how come I didn't feel it when He took it away?"

I stifled a snicker and listened for Larry's response. *This should be good,* I thought.

"Honey, praying is nothing more than talking to God, telling Him what's on your mind," Larry coached tenderly. I couldn't help but think how wise and caring he was in this special moment with his daughter.

I tried hard to swallow the lump that welled up in my throat and stood very still waiting to hear Elizabeth's first heartfelt prayer. *I hope it doesn't involve smiting a certain stepmother,* I thought half-jokingly and half-seriously to myself. Elizabeth was silent for quite awhile and then finally said:

"Hey, God, you want a Popsicle?"

Suddenly, my moist eyes and lumpy throat were chased away by laughter. *Bless your heart, Elizabeth, you always come through with something funny when I least expect it.* I was grateful that her unintentional humor had broken the ice, because I was able to enter the room laughing while Larry was laughing too. *I love to hear him laugh,* I thought.

We closed with a few "thank-you" prayers, and then Larry kissed Elizabeth good night and headed downstairs. I lingered briefly and patted her shoulder. "Good night, cutie," I said.

I usually hate it when Kali tries to hug me or something, but for some reason, tonight I don't really mind that much.

My mood was slightly lighter even though nothing had really changed. Elizabeth's prayer had primed my pump, however, and I slipped into the guest room, sunk into my "prayer chair," and poured out my heart to heaven.

"Lord, I feel guilty and embarrassed by my jealousy over Annette, but Larry never quite seems to grasp *why* I'm jealous. I feel like he's holding on to a past love and failing to fully embrace or appreciate *my* love," I began.

"Lord, he verbally rehashes the past so much that I can barely stand to hear it. I guess he needs to talk about it, or the same subjects wouldn't keep coming up—but I'm his wife, not his counselor. I thought he was ready to move on and begin a new life, but I'm starting to doubt if five years was long enough for him.

"Keeping Annette's memory alive for Elizabeth is one thing, but I feel he crosses that line and enters into longing for his former love! Why can't we learn how to love more than one person at a time in this house?"

I smiled, realizing that God had used Larry's conversation about prayer with Elizabeth to remind me to direct my feelings upward. Ranting to myself only got me more worked up. But when I spewed forth to God, I received comfort. By complaining to Him, I felt heard and understood.

"Lord, you are such a good listener," I praised. "You never interrupt. You always listen and understand without judging or rejecting me for my feelings. Thanks, I really needed a Friend tonight."

After letting the steam out of my emotional kettle, I steeped in silence a good while. I sat with closed eyes and imagined myself in His loving arms. A message came—not one heard audibly with the ears but heard spiritually with the heart: *Be still and know that I am God. You are not in this alone. We are in everything together.*

That was all I needed to hear. Then when I felt calm and at peace, He sent a thought that troubled my soul: *You must make peace with Annette before Larry and Elizabeth can be at peace with their loss.*

He forced me to face the truth: I was trying to fill Annette's void, but the truth was, I never could. I never would be what she was to either of them. It seemed God was urging me to view my role differently. "I don't think I can do that, Lord!" I cried out in confusion, my peace evaporating. "I don't even know how to begin." Fortunately, God knew how.

Though it would be years before I finally came to complete peace with Annette, I found the first step out of this love triangle by thinking back to my beauty contest experiences. During the pageants, when I gazed at the other contestants, I got intimidated, stopped putting my best foot forward, and no longer performed at my full potential. I always saw another girl who was prettier, smarter, or more talented. When I finally accepted that none of that diminished what God had given me, I was able to concentrate on *my* talents and stop focusing on the "competition."

To incorporate those insights into how I dealt with my feelings about Annette, I started by believing that God would help me improve and become a better wife, mother, and friend. I also reframed my idea of what a wife and mother "should be" and focused more on what I *had* rather than on what I *lacked*. I hoped my gifts would become more valuable to Larry and Elizabeth in time. But I came to see that in the Lord's eyes, Annette was different but not better. She gave what she had while she was with them. I must do the same and trust God with the outcome.

If Only I Had Known . . .

- A gentle, reasonable discussion with a child can produce unexpected moments of peace and connection.
- When children and surviving parents experience guilt and feel torn, it doesn't mean they don't love you.
- The "real mom" is not a competitor, but her importance is real and must be dealt with.

What I Would Have Done Differently

I didn't realize how effective it could be to sit down and talk rationally with Elizabeth rather than explode in fiery outbursts at her misbehavior. I wish I'd discovered this a lot sooner! The relationship begins to grow when we get to know our children and allow them to get to know us as "real" people.

I also didn't expect the green-eyed monster to breed such competition between Annette and me. I was trying to fill her shoes, but all I was getting was sore feet! I needed to pitch my predecessor's ballet slippers, lace up my tap shoes, and dance for all I was worth. In God's timing, I learned this lesson—and it wasn't an easy one!

If I had to do it over again, I'd want to have more understanding of the emotional conflict the surviving parent and child struggle with. It is confusing when loyalty to the former spouse/parent collides with the present-day reality of a new wife/mother. If I had been a little more secure with my place in the family, I could have helped Larry and Elizabeth through this struggle rather than adding to it.

I wish I could go back and talk to the "me" of a decade ago. I'd tell her, "Take heart and be patient—this too shall pass."

Reflecting on Your Own Family

- Think back over the last few years and identify some moments of unexpected peace and connection between you and your stepchildren. Did you recognize the moments, and did you savor them?

- What evidence have you seen of the "loyalty struggle" in your husband and stepchildren, and what might you do to help them with this?
- How would you characterize your relationship with the children's mother (or her memory)? Does it need improving?
- What are some things you can do to minimize jealousy of and negative feelings you have about your husband's former wife?

✳ Chapter Six ✳

A Texas Two-Step Right Over the Edge

With the resolve that you are going to make a relationship work,
you can develop peace treaties of love and tolerance and harmony
to transform a difficult situation into something beautiful.
—MAX LUCADO

Thick round tears welled up in my eyes, and a horrible pain gnawed at my heart. I struggled to digest the news that would change my life forever: We were moving to Texas!

It seemed as though we'd just unpacked the last box from our move to Lawrence, even though it had been almost three years. I glanced outside at the small bushes and trees in our landscape that were finally beginning to fill out, and my tears flowed steadily. Even though I initially felt that our family had been blended until our teeth rattled, our home life had ultimately settled into a routine. Now we would be starting all over again, and I was heartbroken.

Why does Kali look so sad? Something's up, and it can't be good; she looks like she's been crying.

"What's wrong, Kali?" Elizabeth asked, with a mixture of curiosity and concern.

"Sit down, honey. I have some news," Larry began.

Elizabeth's eyes widened as she braced for the taste of something unpleasant and searched our eyes for a clue. *I don't have the strength for another tantrum,* I thought, but on hearing the news, Elizabeth reacted unexpectedly. Her response was much like my own: Big tears rolled down her cheeks. She looked like I *felt*—like she'd been kicked in the stomach.

She adequately articulated all of our feelings. "I don't want to move!" she wailed. Her cry was simple anguish, like the sound a heart makes when it breaks. "I just made friends here, I finally like my teacher, and I love my gymnastics team. This isn't fair!" We all agreed. Larry allowed us our grief, and tears flowed without restraint. Elizabeth looked deep into my eyes, reading my pain as easily as I read a bedtime story.

I can't believe this is happening, but at least this time it isn't Kali's fault. She's not the one making us move away. Wow, she's actually sad like me.

The adjustment after our move proved to be a Texas-sized growth step for our sixth-grader. Dallas was topsy-turvy compared to Lawrence. In Kansas, Elizabeth had been an upperclassman in her final year of elementary school; in Texas, she was a middle schooler at the bottom of the heap with seventh- and eighth-graders towering over her. Unfortunately, Elizabeth was also at an age when peers rule and image is everything.

This isn't fair at all! I never even got my sixth-grade graduation party, and I hate those stuck-up seventh- and eighth-graders. Even the sixth-grade kids make fun of me because I don't have a Dooney & Bourke purse or the latest Gap jeans. I've never even heard of this stuff.

As for me, my adjustment was equally hard for different reasons. Larry and I decided I would retire from corporate America and not look for another job in Dallas. For some time, we'd been discussing the idea of me becoming a stay-at-home mom for Elizabeth, and this presented the perfect opportunity. We both believed the decision would take some of the stress off our hectic lifestyle, which it did in some areas, but my stress increased in other ways.

I was grieving from more losses than I could count. In four short years, I had leaped from single life into instant family, and I was struggling to cope with the death of both parents and my little buddy, Pandy. My much-needed support group was left behind in Kansas—another casualty of our relocation.

At least Kali will be home all the time and have milk and cookies ready for me when I get home from school from now on. Since she's not working anymore, she'll have plenty of time to do things at my school. She might even know a thing or two about fashion from her modeling days. Maybe I can talk her into getting me one of those purses.

Without my former career distractions, Larry and Elizabeth expected me to be less frazzled and more available to run errands and chauffeur Elizabeth to and from school activities. But my corporate job was replaced by the seemingly full-time task of getting our family settled into our new digs, and my grief produced its own kind of stress, coupled with an identity crisis I could not adequately articulate.

Eventually, we settled into the Dallas lifestyle, but conflicts with Elizabeth were on the rise.

"Kali, you just widen the gap by using that harsh tone with Elizabeth," Larry said, referring to our most recent confrontation. Our battles often felt like tugs-of-war, and the winner was whoever successfully got Larry on her side. Elizabeth usually walked away with the rope, and I walked away with rope burns.

"Dad, I'm a teenager for goodness sakes! What does Kali think I am — some little baby that needs a sippy cup?" Elizabeth wailed in response to my rule about having no colored beverages on the light-gray carpet.

Somehow, she convinced Larry that she was able to handle drinks without spilling. "That's why they call it a family room — it's where people bond and relax together," he reminded. "Worrying about spills is not very relaxing, Kali. Carpets can be cleaned."

To me, trusting our rambunctious, tumbling Elizabeth with a potentially stain-producing drink on nearly white carpet was a guaranteed disaster, but I kept silent in order to keep the peace.

No sooner had the rules relaxed than Elizabeth had her cup of orange juice sitting on the carpet less than a foot away from where she was tumbling. I seriously doubted that Larry had this combination in mind when he said we should trust her.

"Elizabeth, if that spills, the stain will never come out," I cautioned.

"I'm not going to spill it. I'm careful. Anyway, Dad said I could," Elizabeth said in her best "I won that battle already" tone. The next thing we both knew, the cup was on its side, and the carpet was rapidly turning tangerine. Naturally, I couldn't trust that sticky spill to mere amateurs, so I spent the next hour eradicating the stain.

Why would anyone with a child living at the house choose a nearly white carpet for a family room? The answer should be obvious by now: My design sense was not exactly child-friendly, and I *still* didn't know beans about kids! In my naïveté, I actually thought a few easy-to-follow rules would keep our carpets white. Alas, many of the battle lines I drew related to assaults against my dream home. Many skirmishes might have been avoided had I selected washable walls, darker carpets, and durable stain-resistant furniture. At the time, it didn't fit into my sense of aesthetics and simply didn't occur to me.

Consequently, every day was a showdown at the Schnieders' corral. Elizabeth's irritation with my strict, "dorky" rules was at an all-time high, while my tolerance for her hostile attitude was at an all-time low.

"Whatever!" Elizabeth exclaimed with an eye roll each time I said anything that smacked of correction. She had developed an appalling habit of calling me the "b" word to my face, and frequently I witnessed (and occasionally ducked from) a loaf of bread or a half-eaten apple sailing through the house during her fiery outbursts. Worst of all, I felt powerless to stop her escalating anger and mounting hatred.

I don't have to respect her as a parent. After all, she's not really my mom. She's just making things worse with all these rules. Plus, she has a hard time controlling her temper. And then when she loses it, I can't help it—I just do the same. But she would never dare throw anything at me or call me bad names, so I always win!

Once after scraping apple fragments off of the wall (and discovering the stain could not be repaired without repainting half the room), I raced into the bathroom, turned on the fan so no one would hear, clenched both fists, looked toward heaven, and screamed, "I hate that kid, I hate that kid, I hate that kid!"

"Well, I don't," came the inaudible reply. I found God willing to be my anger sponge, sucking the venom out of my heart before I could deliver a deadly bite. By taking my anger to heaven's gate, I was often calmed and stopped from saying something I would regret.

But lately, even that was not helping. Elizabeth's flare-ups were increasingly frequent, and she had outgrown time-out. I tried grounding and eliminating privileges, but this only fanned her flames and further widened the gap. I was at my wit's end.

To complicate matters, changes at Larry's company required that he do lobbying work at the state capitol. When the legislature was in session (January to June every other year), most of the politicians lived in Austin; consequently, so did my husband.

Thankfully, he was home most weekends. We were delighted to see him pull in the driveway each Friday, but in some ways it actually made our adjustment harder. During the week, Larry was not able to intervene in our squabbles, so we were forced to work things out on our own.

Because Elizabeth was only fourteen, she still relied on me for transportation. Therefore, if I didn't like her vocabulary or her attitude, I simply refused to drive *anywhere* until she cleaned up her act. We fought like she-wolves, but she soon learned that if she pushed me, she would be scrambling to find another driver.

My newly discovered upper hand didn't necessarily curtail her trash talk, but it worked wonders on my self-respect. I had made friends with a few mothers, and I quickly learned that mother-daughter verbal battles were the rule and not the exception during the teenage years. *Wow,* I thought, *I've been beating myself up for nothing! These mothers have the same problems, only they don't second-guess their decisions or worry about their inadequacies like I do. Some of them don't enjoy or even like their children all the time, and they are real birth moms!*

What a relief! I stopped worrying about our arguments and refused to be bothered by Elizabeth's regular reminders that I was "*not* the Mama" and that I was hated. As Bette Davis said, "If you've never been hated by your child, you've never been a parent."[2]

I also noticed that when Larry was away, Elizabeth asked *me* to help her study for a test and regularly invited me to watch television programs. Thursday became "our night."

There seemed to be a pattern developing: Elizabeth misbehaved; I decided upon a consequence. When she got mad and threw a fit, I didn't back down. The more committed I was to the consequence, the more quickly the gap narrowed. It's almost as though she were waiting to see if I cared enough to say no and stand my ground.

But soon the weekend rolled around, Larry returned, and the bickering resumed.

"Dad, Kali's ruining my birthday," Elizabeth whined. "She won't let me do *anything* fun. I want a really cool Hawaiian swim party, and she's going to turn it into a big fat flop." She called forth her very best crocodile tears, which amazingly Larry didn't realize were manufactured for their persuasive effect.

Sometimes I have to pull out my "secret weapon." I know that if at first I don't get my way, cry, cry again!

"Nobody's gonna come to the babyish, boring party she wants me to have!" Elizabeth continued. "She's going to embarrass me in front of all my friends."

"Larry, that's not true," I chimed in. "I told her we could have the Hawaiian party; I'm just not sure about having it at home. And when I suggested we limit the guests to ten girls, Elizabeth called me the 'b' word. After that I refused to discuss the party further."

Larry frowned at the mention of her swearing habit, but he turned to me and asked, "What's the matter with having it here?"

"First of all, she wants twenty girls, and that's too many in the pool at one time. I can't possibly keep an eye on all of them and also provide the food and games! Plus, they'll be dripping water throughout the house, and we don't need all the floors and furniture soaked with water," I lamented.

"See!" Elizabeth howled. "She cares more about her stupid furniture than about her own daughter!"

So now you're my daughter, I thought, *and it's not even laundry day.*

"Good grief! Seven years together, and you're still at it. I've been fighting in Austin all week, and then I come home to The Family Feud. Democrats and Republicans get along better! Come on, Kali. Let's not widen the gap over a little pool party. Can't we please have some harmony tonight?" he said.

Seeking a compromise, Larry suggested we have the Hawaiian party at home but that we limit the invitations to twelve guests. "A win-win," he said.

I enjoyed shopping with Elizabeth for the party accessories. We found adorable grass skirts, colorful leis, and flowers for the girls' hair. "A few festive balloons, a birthday cake with palm trees and a hula girl, and we're all set," I said. Elizabeth beamed.

Kali can be fun sometimes. My dad would never let me get all this cool stuff for my party. If she weren't here, I might end up making the grass skirts out of old newspapers or something. Not only that, I'm beginning to like just being around her. She might not hate me as much as I thought.

When party day arrived, we got off to a rousing start with a scavenger hunt. It was a precious sight: twelve grass skirts racing through our neighborhood to gather the items on their list. It was going fine, and I felt slightly guilty about not having wanted the party at the house.

The boisterous hula girls soon burst in the door with their loot. Then they rushed out to the pool like a school of minnows. Thinking I was being a very discreet lifeguard, I settled into the family room so I could keep an eye out for any dangerous behavior. The girls noticed me, and pretty soon Elizabeth ran in to object.

"Kali, you're wrecking everything. Don't sit around watching us. Can't you go in your bedroom or something?" Elizabeth complained.

"Honey, I'm responsible for everyone's safety. I should be in here where I can help if needed," I explained.

"Well, you're *not* needed. Da-aaaaad!" she screamed.

Larry came in to calm the rising tide, and I felt like a bad child being dragged from the party by my ear. "Kali, the girls are fine. I'll keep an eye on them. Don't hang around gawking at them. Remember when you were fourteen?" Larry asked, trying to shame me out of the family room.

"I certainly *do* remember, which is why I'm here," I protested. While I suspected that Larry's idea of "keeping an eye on them" involved setting up a putting green in the loft and wandering downstairs every hour or so for a Coke, against my better judgment I retreated to our bedroom. Of course, I was able to hibernate for only about thirty minutes before the girls' excited squeals aroused my curiosity and I went out to take a peek.

When I rounded the corner, my jaw dropped a foot. I was just in time to see a guest scooping handfuls of sod from the puddle she had made in our yard with the garden hose. She flung the sod on another girl, and suddenly muddy grass was flying in all directions.

While I realize parents are supposed to be raising children, not Fescue grass, seeing our freshly seeded and impossible-to-grow lawn being ripped out by its little roots was more than I could take! I ran outside as though my hair were on fire, roughly grabbed the instigator by the arm, and said something "tender" like, "What's the matter with you? How'd you like me to call your mother?"

What a pretty party picture: I was screeching, Elizabeth was mortified, Larry was furious because I had embarrassed her, and the guests agreed I was the meanest mother any of them knew. The party that started with a bang ended with a whimper—my whimper. Elizabeth summarily banned me from any future parties, including her wedding.

I knew she'd ruin everything. How could she do this to me? By Monday everyone at school will hear how awful my party was and how dorky my parents are. Now I know for sure that Kali hates me. She doesn't even want me to have any friends!

When Larry left for Austin on Monday, Elizabeth and I still were not speaking. My stomach was upset, and my head was throbbing from trying all weekend to sort out who was right and who was wrong in the party fiasco. I felt like the victim of a hidden-camera television program. *If only someone would jump out of the bushes and tell me this was all a joke,* I thought.

Once again my flair for the dramatic had created a lose-lose situation. Yet no matter how many times I rehashed the scene in my mind, I remained perplexed. Maybe I should have taken some of my mother's advice: "It's not *what* you say, Kali; it's *how* you say it." Perhaps a softer approach would have saved the lawn *and* my daughter's party. On the other hand, part of me felt justified, even if I had overreacted. What homeowner is going to stand by and watch while a group of teenagers intentionally rips the yard to shreds? The more I tried to sort this out, the worse my head pounded. *I need an impartial advisor who is not emotionally involved,* I thought. But it didn't immediately occur to me to take the problem to the one Counselor who could have helped.

That afternoon when I picked up Elizabeth from school, she climbed in the car, slammed the door, and blurted out, "You ruined my reputation! All the kids think that *I'm* a big dork and that *you're* a monster—and they're right!"

I let her vent and kept myself calm with visions of lying with a cold towel on my brow. When we got home, the phone was ringing. It was Larry.

Elizabeth started laying it on pretty thick: "Dad, how many stupid things does Kali have to do for you to realize she is *not* the right person to be my mom?" Elizabeth cried. "That woman you married hates me, and now so do all the kids at school."

I waited for Elizabeth to wind up her accusations so I could have my own chat with Larry. I began with something I hoped would generate sympathy. "I've got a splitting headache. I don't even feel up to driving Elizabeth to gymnastics this afternoon," I explained, but before I could tell Larry that I had arranged a ride with another mother, Elizabeth reacted.

She's still mad about the party, so she's refusing to take me to gymnastics. She's trying to pay me back for getting her in trouble with Dad. First she ruins my party, and now she wants to ruin my entire life. I have to be at practice tonight; I've got an important meet coming up!

"I hate you!" she screamed.

"Honey, let me call you back," I said, hoping to get off the phone and straighten this out without Larry overhearing and trying to referee from the office. All of a sudden, Elizabeth dug all ten fingernails into my arm as it rested on the back of the couch. The pain was so unexpected and sharp that I had no time to think; I simply reacted. "Ouch, stop that!" I screamed as I came down across her arm with a swift whack from the phone receiver still resting in my other hand.

"Ouch!" Elizabeth shrieked. "That's child abuse!" I was devastated: I had become the wicked stepmother after all. Then Elizabeth turned to me and said with sickening self-assurance, "I know how to get rid of you anytime I want. This was just a warning."

I sure wish I could get rid of her. Maybe if I keep this up, she'll leave on her own. Wouldn't that be great? Then I'd have my dad all to myself and not have to deal with her being so mean all the time.

I hated myself for allowing things to get so out of hand, and I feared what might happen if things kept escalating. When Larry returned home, I pleaded with him.

"We should seek professional help. Elizabeth's anger is out of control."

He was looking at the bruise on her arm. "I'd say *you* were out of control," he observed.

"I was protecting myself!" I protested. "She's strong, and she dug her nails into my skin hard enough to draw blood. Just look at the cuts on my arm! And it's *not* the first time she's done this," I reminded him as the memory of a former fingernail assault resurfaced.

"Well, did you provoke her?" he countered.

"I definitely did *not* provoke her, and nothing justifies a physical attack."

But Larry just wanted the hostility to stop. He still didn't think we all needed counseling but agreed I could go if I felt it would help.

I had a good long cry and an even longer talk with God. After pouring out my confusion and hurt, I admitted that I could no longer cope by prayer alone. "Lord, help us," I cried. "I'm terrified by these violent outbursts. I need someone who will listen and give suggestions—toss out some new things to try with Elizabeth," I pleaded. "If You *are* giving me the wisdom I need, I'm just not getting it. Please lead me to a counselor who has the right solutions. Even if Larry and Elizabeth don't go, any positive changes I make might help them too. We can't go on this way," I concluded.

It was as though God were just waiting for me to ask. He led me to Jodi, the family counselor I credit with keeping me sane, married, and out of prison.

If Only I Had Known . . .

- Often it's not *what* you say but *how* you say it that determines the outcome.
- One of the most reassuring discoveries a stepmom can make is that even "real" mothers sometimes struggle to get along with their children.

What I Would Have Done Differently

I wish I'd learned sooner how to pick my battles, control my temper, and use an effective tone of voice when I was upset. The birthday party incident showed me just how out of my control the situation was. If I had a do-over on that one, I would still put an end to the girls' mischief, but I'd do it in a calm, reasonable way. Better yet, I might have just turned the situation over to Larry. If we'd been supervising the party, the shredding of the lawn never would have happened.

If I had known how helpful it would be to get involved with other parents, I would have made friends with other moms much earlier in my parenting career! Once I finally started talking with the mothers, I learned I was not alone in my struggles. This single fact calmed me immensely. I was able to see which conflicts were common, and I gained the resolve to set boundaries and determine "nonnegotiables." Talking with other parents also gave me ideas and approaches that never would have dawned on me.

Reflecting on Your Own Family

- Can you think of situations that would have turned out better if you'd handled them differently? In hindsight, what would you change about your behavior?
- How has the ability (or lack of ability) to effectively "choose battles" been a factor in your parenting journey?

- How has your involvement with other parents and stepparents been helpful to you?
- What could you do to increase the support and ideas you exchange with other mothers and further deepen your friendships with them?

✳ Chapter Seven ✳

Missteps in the Laundry Room of Life

*Let us not lose heart in doing good, for in due time
we will reap if we do not grow weary.*
—GALATIANS 6:9

I felt such guilt as I poured out the details of the heartbreaking
fingernail/phone altercation and our general family trauma to Jodi.
She had a way of helping me see the unseen, love the unlovely, and
keep my self-worth intact through the involved process of untangling
this knotted twine. Through Jodi, God provided sound guidance and
a detached perspective that enabled me to hold on, hang in, and shape
up.

Jodi helped me see that I was not very good at picking my battles
(in *my* mind, every skirmish required heavy artillery) and then pre-
scribed a solution: "During those times you feel compelled to force
a particular outcome, try backing off and letting the natural consequences happen." In other words, rather than react immediately, I
needed to cool off and develop a well-thought-out plan.

Using the orange juice incident as an example of my tendency
to "fix" things before they were broken, Jodi helped me see how my

actions were drawing fire from Larry and Elizabeth: "I'm wondering what would happen if you didn't make a "no drinks on the carpet" rule. What if you had kept silent and waited to see if a spill happened and then stepped back and let Elizabeth or Larry fix the problem?" Jodi asked wisely.

"Well, then I'd have an orange stain on the carpet because neither of them would clean it properly," I said, a little confused. "Orange juice is impossible to get out, you know."

"Yes. But what would happen if you didn't get it out?" Jodi prodded.

"Well, I guess we'd buy new carpet or live with it stained," I offered, still perplexed.

"And who is in the doghouse then? If Larry pays to clean or replace the carpet very often, eventually he will make a rule, or maybe Elizabeth will learn to be more careful. Either way, no one can shift the issue onto you."

I took every word to heart and strived to implement Jodi's suggestions. Once I saw how my "ounce of prevention" philosophy was adding to our problems instead of preventing them, Jodi was able to help me set boundaries and let others live with the consequences of their behavior.

I was also spending some quality time with my Divine Counselor, who affirmed Jodi's approach. I was amazed during a morning devotional to discover a verse I'd never seen before: "In quietness and trust is your strength" (Isaiah 30:15). So I memorized it and vowed to stop ignoring the spiritual nudges that urged me to go against my nature.

At times I bit my tongue until it bled, but slowly, knot by twisted knot, our tangle began to straighten out a bit. Thank goodness, because it wasn't too long before I had a real doozy of a chance to put my new strategy to the test!

It was nearly eleven when my tennis match ended. Even though I knew Elizabeth might still be sleeping, I grabbed the cell phone and dialed the number. I was excited to share the news of my stellar accomplishment.

"Good morning, Elizabeth," I said in a cheery voice. It was always risky sharing tidbits of true significance with my daughter; I never knew what reaction to expect. Depending on her mood, Elizabeth's comments could range from an upbeat "That's cool!" all the way to a deadpan "So, big deal." But most frequently, I heard silence.

Feeling adventurous, I pressed on. "Hey, guess who won her match!" I announced, oozing with pride.

"Way to go! What was the score?" Elizabeth asked with uncharacteristic interest.

I know how important those stupid tennis matches are to Kali, so a little sucking up can't hurt. Besides, I need a favor.

How odd for Elizabeth to be so enthusiastic about my tennis match, I thought. *Hmmm, she must want something.* My cynicism was born out of many similar conversations with this child who usually had no money of her own and constantly wanted some from me. However, money wasn't foremost on Elizabeth's mind at the moment. My suspicions about her motives were quickly confirmed, nonetheless.

Elizabeth asked sweetly, "Can Matt come over?"

I sure hope Kali says yes. Matt's phone call woke me up so early this morning that I must have been a little out of it. I wasn't thinking clearly when I said it was okay if he came over, but I couldn't let Kali's stupid ideas about not having boys in the house when she's not home stop me from impressing him. If I would have told Matt not to have his dad drop him off because of some stupid rule, he'd think I was a nerd! Maybe if I get Kali's permission now, she'll never know I already intended to break the rule.

Elizabeth's new "boyfriend" was handsome, charming, polite, and the first young man on the scene to cause a bleep on my motherly radar screen. He had come over one evening to do homework with Elizabeth, but until then, her interaction with boys had been limited to a phone conversation or a specific school function, like the big dance. Well, the dance moved on, but Matt didn't.

During the homework session, I noticed that Matt was a little too friendly. His affection was not exactly inappropriate, but this young man certainly seemed at ease touching Elizabeth, and I was not at ease with this development. I thought boy-girl relationships were supposed to be awkward at their age; this smooth kid was a mother's nightmare!

Nevertheless, Larry frequently cautioned me not to create a problem with Elizabeth by saying no whenever yes was possible. So I swallowed my concern and replied, "Of course, Matt is welcome to come by after lunch when I'm home. Right now I'm running errands, and then I'll stop at Wendy's to pick up our lunch. What would you like to eat?" I asked.

Oh no, I'm busted—Kali's coming home for lunch. She's supposed to eat lunch with her stupid tennis friends and gab all day. Matt was supposed to come, swim, and leave without her ever suspecting a thing. Kali would just have a cow if she knew he was already on his way over. Now I'll have to tell him about the stupid rules and figure out something so we don't get caught. This is a disaster! Kali's really blowing my major shot at popularity.

Ignoring my food question, Elizabeth demanded to know exactly when I would be home.

"When my errands are finished." I replied.

"What errands? How long will that take?" she asked, her tone growing more agitated.

"Probably an hour or so. Now, what do you want to eat?" I asked, noticing my tone and Elizabeth's were similar now.

Elizabeth placed her order: "I'll have the kids' meal, plain junior hamburger, fries, a small Coke, and a Frosty."

"You want the toy?" I teased.

She's such a geek. It's time for a new tactic. Maybe I can still salvage this situation by making Kali feel guilty about putting our lives on hold for her own convenience!

"We aren't waiting all day while you shop. We're just going to lay out in the sun. What's the big deal?" Elizabeth demanded, her tone turning hostile.

Technically, we won't even be breaking your stupid rule if we aren't inside the house.

Lay out in the sun? That involves swimsuits! I thought with my overly protective attitude on red alert. Confident that Larry was in agreement, I firmly reminded Elizabeth of the rule: "No boys unless I'm home—period."

Why did Dad have to marry such a monster? My real mom never would have treated me this way. I won't put up with this.

"Well, Matt's coming over now, and we'll just sit outside until you get here. That good enough for you, Kali?" she snapped.

"Nope, not even close," I retorted. "No means *no,* Elizabeth. If you keep up the attitude, Matt won't be coming at all!"

How does she do it? I thought. *That girl skyrockets me from blissful peace into war mode with one little phone call!*

The next words to come from Elizabeth's mouth definitely sent my blood pressure into the upper stratosphere. She screamed at full volume, "You are such a . . . !"

"That little snot hung up on me! I won't tolerate such disrespect!" I screeched after the phone line went dead.

I remembered the day I hung up on my own mother; it happened *only* once. Not so with Elizabeth. Hanging up on me was her favorite power play. Elizabeth's disconnect was designed with precision timing to prevent me from hearing the horrid name she called me, but I could easily fill in the blank with the full measure of contempt the missing word conveyed. Elizabeth's hanging-up habit ignited a response in me much like dumping a gallon of lighter fluid directly onto hot coals in the ol' hibachi. *Kaboom!*

But now I had two secret weapons: God and Jodi. "Quietness is your strength" had become my mantra, and I combined it with Jodi's tip of the month, "Cool off and develop a plan." Thankfully, I could hear their voices ringing in my ears, urging me to respond rather than merely react. Otherwise, I was so furious over Elizabeth's disrespectful phone etiquette that I might have missed the "nudge" from above warning me that something even *more* crucial was awry on the home front.

Fortunately, the nudge was persistent. I skipped the errands, flipped a U-turn, wheeled into the Wendy's drive-through, grabbed that kids' meal, floored the accelerator, and flew toward home like a heat-seeking missile.

Matt and I had better skip the swimming. If we stay inside the house and listen for the garage door to open, we'll have enough warning time for Matt to escape out the back gate.

My tires squealed as I rounded the corner and stopped abruptly on the visitors' side of our subdivision entrance. I attempted to calm my voice and greet our favorite gatekeeper. "Hey, Homer," I called nonchalantly, "I was wondering if we've had any visitors come through today."

Homer innocently responded, unaware of the megaton blast his statement would generate. "Yes. Mr. Matt is here."

Mustering an artificial smile and using every last ounce of composure, I asked the killer question: "Oh, really? How long ago did Mr. Matt arrive?"

"About fifteen minutes," Homer explained.

Homer barely got the words out before I hit the gas. I wish I could say I prayed a lofty prayer for guidance and bent my knees in search of heaven's wisdom, but I did not. Prayer, however, would have been the only thing that could save Elizabeth from the approaching wrath of this mom on a mission.

Adrenaline pumped through me so rapidly and in such a quantity that I instantly identified with all the mothers who reportedly raise automobile wheels off of trapped babies. I hastily formulated a motherly action plan: I would rescue our daughter's reputation from the clutches of the Don Juan of Middle School; then I would strangle her.

I suspected and confirmed to my smug satisfaction that the padlock from our backyard gate had been removed. I rapidly deduced that the scheme depended upon Matt's fast-break getaway. I figured Elizabeth would listen for the garage door, giving Matt plenty of time to dart out the back door, through the backyard, and out the back gate. After an appropriate lapse of time, Matt would arrive at our front door in full accordance with the house rules—*after* I was home.

Oh, they were clever, but not quite clever enough. Thanks to Jodi, I had a plan! Opting for a sneak attack, I had no intention of announcing my arrival by using the garage door opener. The picture of stealth, I pulled up in front of our house, leaped from the car, and slipped in the front door.

The click of the dead bolt opening gave me away, and I could hear the sound of kitchen chairs scraping against the ceramic tile. Elizabeth and Matt scrambled to execute their escape strategy but apparently had failed to enact a dry run. Matt was startled to the point of panic. He stumbled from his chair, missed the back door, and mistakenly tore down the hall into our laundry room—a dead end.

Meanwhile, I rounded the corner, assessed the kitchen situation, and demanded an answer from Elizabeth: "All right, where is he?"

Her deer-in-the-headlights look was priceless; she blinked three or four times with her mouth gaping and pointed toward the laundry room.

Oh man, I'm in deep doo-doo now!

I handed Elizabeth the kids' meal, ordered her to sit down and eat, and then marched down the hall to the laundry room. I opened the door and instantly knew where Matt was hiding. In a room equipped with a sink, a washer and dryer, and an open closet space for hanging clothes to drip-dry, there was one obvious option. Unless Larry's golf pants had grown tennis shoes, there was a boy in our laundry.

I stood in front of the drip closet a little while for effect. When Matt made no move after about three minutes (which must have seemed like thirty to him), I cleared my throat and waited again. Still no movement emanated from among the shirts and shorts.

At long last I called, "Maaaaatt." I pronounced his name with all of the voice inflection at my command.

"Yes, ma'am," he said sheepishly.

"You may come out now," I spoke slowly, deliberately, and with surprising anger management. *This is even more effective than yelling,* I thought to myself as I witnessed the look of sheer terror. Caught red-handed—this was rare!

Often when I approached Larry with a complaint based solely on my intuition, his reply was, "Did you *see* her do this? Then how do you know what happened?" Common sense would indicate the culprit because there were only three people living in our house, and one of *us* had to be the offender. Blaming it on Pandy would no longer work—the poor dog died years ago!

I walked Matt to the door, announcing to Elizabeth, "Matt and I are leaving now. Please say goodbye."

"Well, I'm coming too!" she shot back.

"No, Elizabeth, you sit down, eat your lunch, and remain in that chair until I get back. *Then* we are going to have a nice long talk."

My life is over. Everyone at school is going to hear about this and think I'm a dork for having such a mean "mother." I can't imagine what evil things Kali will say to totally destroy my relationship with Matt! I just know he'll never talk to me again. The witch wouldn't even let me ride along. I hate her!

By the time I got outside, Matt had scooted into the backseat of my car. "Oh no, son," I said as I took my place behind the wheel. "You need to sit up here with me." I could almost hear a gulp from Matt as he unbuckled his seat belt and reluctantly moved to the passenger seat. I put the car in gear, asked Matt where he lived, and headed toward his house.

"Now, Matt," I began, "as Elizabeth's good friend, you need to understand and obey the rules of our house. Today I am going to assume you were unaware of the rules and therefore did not break them intentionally. Am I right?" I asked.

"Yes, ma'am," Matt said with his eyes fixed out the car window.

"Elizabeth knows we don't allow boys in our home when Mr. Schnieders and I are gone, nor do we allow Elizabeth to visit her friends' houses when parents aren't around," I explained.

"I understand. We have that same rule at home, Mrs. Schnieders," said Matt reassuringly.

I was relieved to know that Matt had thoughtful parents who saw eye-to-eye with us on this important safeguard. My tone softened slightly. "Good, Matt. I'm really glad to know that you understand the importance of rules and further understand that no true friend would *ever* encourage Elizabeth to break a rule. Anyone who would do such a thing is not really a friend and would not be a welcome guest. That's not so hard to understand, is it, Matt?" I asked.

"No, Mrs. Schnieders. I'm sorry," Matt said convincingly.

I felt a little guilty being so hard on Matt, because deep down I believed he was a good boy—but even good boys have hormones and can wind up in trouble without noticing the danger signals. That's why God created mothers. There would be *no* raging hormones in our house on *my* watch!

My stomach is in knots. I think I might even puke. I'll bet Kali's really yelling at Matt by now. How does she do it? One minute I'm having the time of my life, the next minute I'm furious, and now I'm totally scared out of my mind. Sure wish I could get a redo on this day!

I'd better get my new made-up story straight before Kali gets back and starts yelling at me. I could just sob and apologize—that works sometimes. I hate lying, on top of everything, but I've dug myself a hole too deep for the truth this time. Unless I come up with a good excuse, I'll probably be grounded for the rest of my life.

I was quite certain Elizabeth would be on the phone with Matt for a full report before I returned, but when I walked into the kitchen, I was stunned to see her sitting in her chair as I had commanded. The drive with Matt also enabled me to get my fury further under control and speak with calm authority.

"Now, Kali, I can explain this whole thing," Elizabeth began.

"Oh, I am *ready* to hear this," I said, pulling up a chair across from her at the table. Elizabeth produced the crocodile tears and fake sob she frequently used on Larry when attempting to squirm out of punishment. I never was swayed by her dramatics, so I listened intently to each of the "explanations" Elizabeth concocted and allowed her to elaborate fully. After each fabrication, I simply responded, "Now let me tell you why *that* one doesn't work." Then I'd reveal bits of the botched escape plan that I had deduced. Elizabeth appeared mesmerized by my apparent clairvoyant abilities.

"Now would you like me to tell you what you're *thinking,*

Elizabeth?" I asked with a slight smile.

She shrugged her shoulders.

"You're wondering why we have such a dumb rule as 'No boys in the house,' right?" I asked.

Her eyes widened. "How'd you know that?"

"Because the same question was running through my mind when my mother taught the rule to me," I explained.

Elizabeth looked at me with a strange expression I couldn't interpret. Genuine tears were now trickling down her soft cheeks. She made no objections and no smart remarks. Sensing I was on some sort of parental roll, I continued.

"Elizabeth, I was a good kid, and I thought my mother was judging me unfairly. It hurt to think that my own mother didn't trust me and might even be questioning my morals. But she explained that trusting me was not the problem but that it was the situation that caused her concern. She was protecting my reputation from the watchful eyes of neighbors who might draw the wrong conclusions if I were entertaining boys while home alone."

As we talked, I hoped Elizabeth might come to view my rules as lessons passed down to me from my mother. I wanted so much for Elizabeth to see that the very disciplines she hated so much were really warnings of love from a stepmother who cared too much to overlook behavior that would have harmful consequences if left unchecked. *How can I make her understand that rules are to protect her from herself and others? What must I do to convince her that rules aren't things I think up to spoil her fun, embarrass her, or exercise control? I wonder if she'll ever see me as anything but an evil woman out to do her harm.*

Elizabeth's head hung low. For a rare moment, she was faced with parental correction and showed no signs of bolting from the room as was her customary response. It seemed as though I could "feel" her repentant heart beating in time with my own. *I wonder if this is how it feels to God when my heart has broken and I'm sorry for my mistakes*, I mused.

I continued speaking with a softer voice: "It's very difficult to restore a good reputation once it's lost, Elizabeth. My job is to protect you inside this house, even if I can't control what you do when you leave home. That's where trust comes in. I believe you have good moral values, but I also know that when a girl and boy are alone, things can get out of control rather quickly. I don't want you to wind up in a situation you're not equipped to handle, and if I'm home, that can't happen. I *want* you to blame me when your friends criticize you for saying no. I don't want you to be labeled a dork, but I don't mind if they call me one. They're my rules, not yours."

Elizabeth asked if she could be excused to the bathroom.

If I take my time, maybe she'll get tired of waiting for me and move on to something else.

When Elizabeth emerged, I was still sitting at the table. "Now let's talk consequences," I said. "First, you intentionally disobeyed and then lied to cover it up. You also called me a hateful name and tried to disguise it by hanging up on me."

I let the weight of the offenses hang in the air. "What do you think the consequences should be for these poor choices?" I asked.

Elizabeth wiped her eyes, blew her nose, and replied, "No television, telephone, or computer for a week?"

"Lying is *very* serious and demands a heavy consequence, in my book," I continued solemnly. "Elizabeth, if it were up to me, you would be grounded from *everything* for a *month*. That's what my mother did when I broke a major rule."

Elizabeth gasped audibly and began to sob. Her glower conveyed her disdain for my idea of fair punishment, but she said nothing. I interpreted this as another signal of progress, so I went for broke.

"I know pretty well how this will play out," I continued. "The minute your father comes home tonight, you'll cry your best crocodile tears. You'll swear this was all a big misunderstanding, and you'll probably be grounded for a few days and then slide back into your regular routine. You won't benefit from this experience, though, because if the lesson isn't costly, it usually isn't learned.

Elizabeth fumed in silence, but her eyes said a mouthful.

"One thing is different this time, though. You know what *I* think is the right thing to do, and you know why. So unless you have something more to say, I guess we're finished," I concluded.

Elizabeth seethed with anger and ran sobbing to her room. The house was very quiet for the rest of the afternoon—until Larry walked in the door from work. "How are my two angels?" he called from the entryway.

No one spoke, and tension hung in the room like a wet velvet drape. Larry looked quizzically at me as I stood in the kitchen making dinner. Finally I sighed and offered, "All the angels flew the coop."

We heard a giggle from Elizabeth's room. *Here it comes,* I thought. I rolled my eyes and braced for an Academy Award–winning performance.

"What's going on around here?" Larry asked, perplexed. By now, Elizabeth had appeared in the kitchen.

"Well, it looks as though I'm grounded for a month," she said in a strangely upbeat tone.

"A month! What could you have possibly done to deserve that?" Larry asked in disbelief.

I simply shrugged and allowed Elizabeth to have the floor. By now we'd all gathered at the kitchen table, and Elizabeth told the story in every truthful detail. Larry was stunned; I was more so.

"Yeah, I guess you could say that Kali and I bonded," Elizabeth concluded.

I choked back the lump in my throat. The glorious words dripped like long-awaited honey from my daughter's lips. Occasionally, we catch a glimpse of heaven—a frozen moment when we are keenly aware that years of praying have combined into a single heartbeat and the prayer is answered. We dare not breathe for fear the scene will vanish. We want to press the "save" button on the memory of our hearts, capture the glorious glow within, and revel in the evidence at hand that God is with us—listening, caring, and leading. Elizabeth and I had bonded, and I wasn't even aware.

She rose from her chair and sweetly asked, "Kali, can I have a hug?"

I trembled and lightly placed my arms around her shoulders, waiting for her familiar recoil. This was the first time since our wedding that Elizabeth permitted my affectionate touch. "That felt so good! Can I have another one?" Elizabeth asked, fully accepting the hugs my arms longed to deliver.

Our journey was so tiresome and overgrown with skepticism on both sides. When I had almost given up hope that our hearts would ever bond, we rounded a bend, and suddenly I discovered we were right on course, taking one divinely guided goose step after another.

The wicked stepmother label that had covered me for years like an ugly garment simply slipped from my shoulders and fell to the kitchen floor. Every eye roll, insult, and rejection previously hurled at my heart no longer mattered.

If Only I Had Known . . .

- It's normal for a stepparent's rules and suggestions to be resented, so often a better course of action is to keep quiet, pray, and allow natural consequences to occur.
- Our strength comes from being "quiet" and trusting the Lord, not from jumping in to fix everything.
- A difficult parenting situation can have a successful outcome if you give yourself time to cool off and develop a plan.

What I Would Have Done Differently

Jodi's suggestions and my determination to carry them out really changed the course of my relationship with Elizabeth. For the first time, I felt as though I had the tools to handle her behavior appropriately, without engaging in screaming matches and physical skirmishes. I was so thankful God was teaching me these lessons, even though they seemed to be a little late in coming! However, I trust in His timing, and I probably wasn't ready for the lessons before reaching the end of my rope. It wasn't until I desperately cried out to Him for help that I was led to Jodi. In retrospect, I definitely wish I'd made that anguished call to God a few years sooner!

Reflecting on Your Own Family

- Can you think of situations in which your warnings and rules have done more harm than good?
- How difficult would it be for you to step back from your need to be the authority and let members of your family experience natural consequences? Do you sense a need to try this?
- What recent situations would have had better outcomes if you'd been able to cool off and develop a plan?
- What could you do right now to begin incorporating a "calmer, gentler" approach to parenting?

* *Chapter Eight* *

Three Cheers for a Step Forward

Life . . . would give her everything of consequence, life would shape
her, not we. All we were good for was to make the introductions.
—HELEN HAYES

Gymnastics had always been the center of the Schnieders' world—until
the world tilted. As Elizabeth prepared to enter the ninth grade, a growth
spurt impacted her performance and prevented her from competing past
Junior Olympic level nine. Although Elizabeth was initially resistant to
the idea, her friend Mandy convinced her to try cheerleading.

Once Elizabeth was bitten by the cheerleading bug, her passion
to make the squad quickly became an obsession—so much so that I
began to wonder if her driven "spirit" was in some way connected to
the cheerleading legacy her mother had left.

I absolutely have to make cheerleader. Then I'll finally be part of the "in"
crowd. If my mother could do it, so can I! Dad will be so proud of me for fol-
lowing in her footsteps.

Maybe if she accomplishes this goal, she'll feel connected with her mother and find a sense of peace, I mused as I drove Elizabeth to school for the tryouts. I chatted breezily on unrelated topics, hoping to distract her from the competition ahead, but she was silent and non-communicative. We both knew how much she wished that her father were not in Austin on this important day and that *he* were driving her to school. Nevertheless, I was glad to fill in and offer the best pep talk my inadequacy could muster. I reached over, squeezed her hand, and predicted that her years of dedication were about to pay off.

Man, I wish my real mom were here. She would be able to give me some good advice. Even my dad knows just the right things to say when I'm nervous. But no, I'm stuck with Kali.

"Don't worry. Just do your best, have fun, and smile pretty" was how I paraphrased the advice I heard Larry give before many gymnastics meets. I tossed in the tip about smiling as a remnant of the counsel my mom had provided during my beauty pageant competitions.

I don't know what hole Kali has been living in, but cheerleading isn't what it used to be. I can't just jump around flashing a big smile and expect to make the squad.

Elizabeth rolled her eyes, giving me the signal that Larry's advice sounded dorky coming from me. Oh, well. Deep down I believed that at the end of this day, we would celebrate her achievement together.

I've never cheered before, but I learned all the jumps and dances in my years of gymnastics. Although I don't know anything about the "spirit" stuff, I'm the only girl trying out who can do a standing backflip. I'm nervous about performing in front of the student body for the popularity vote, but the judges will be impressed by the difficulty of my tumbling. I'm sure I'll make the squad!

Later that afternoon when the tryouts were over, I sat in the car and waited for Elizabeth to burst into view. I watched expectantly for her beaming smile and glanced at the pretty bouquet of daisies waiting in the backseat to congratulate our little cheerleader. So often in the past, this clueless mother-wannabe had failed to produce the appropriate posies, but this time I was pleased with myself for being on top of things and grateful that Susan, my mothering mentor, had tipped me off about cheerleading tryouts being one of "those" occasions.

Elizabeth finally emerged, but her face was void of the exuberance I anticipated. Still, knowing how Elizabeth liked to pretend she'd gotten bad grades only to produce an all-As report card, I deduced that she was enjoying the torture her silence created for me. "So, how'd it go?" I asked, smiling broadly as I waited for her to notice the daisies, her favorite flower.

"I didn't make it," Elizabeth said, void of any telltale emotion.

"Oh, come on. Don't tease me," I replied, mindful of the knots growing in my stomach.

"I'm *not* kidding. I didn't make it!" she cried as giant tears rolled down her cheeks. Then between heart-wrenching sobs, Elizabeth told me about the painful way the girls learned the outcome of their tryout.

"After waiting *forever,* the cheer coaches had us all sit in a big circle. We had to close our eyes with our hands behind our back while they walked around giving us envelopes. When everyone had one, we opened our eyes and read the names of the chosen squad inside the envelope. I read the ten names as fast as I could, but everyone was screaming and yelling like crazy. I read the list three times! I kept hoping there had been some mistake, but . . ." Her raspy voice trailed off into agonized weeping. "It was so embarrassing!"

Dear Lord, help me know what to say, I prayed as I kicked myself for my initial reaction. I could only imagine how devastated Elizabeth felt. Although I had firsthand knowledge from my high school musical tryouts that rejection is survivable and far from a tragedy, this was still very painful for both of us. I tried to comfort her, but my earlier comment had put a chasm between us. She would have none of my soothing. It was an excruciating drive.

When we got home, Elizabeth ran to her room and slammed the door. I didn't even mind; I wanted to slam one myself. As the evening wore on, I knocked on her door a few times, hoping to offer encouragement, but each attempt was rebuffed. I felt utterly helpless. I wanted to rock her in my arms and have a good cry together, but sadly we wound up aching in isolation all evening, sharing our tears with our pillows rather than with each other.

When Larry called at bedtime to congratulate his girl, I broke the news as gently as I could, explaining the way she was informed and her reaction to the rejection. "She's been crying in her room ever since we got home. She didn't want any dinner. When I knock on her door, she tells me to leave her alone. I know she's heartbroken. I want to help, but I don't know how."

"Tell her I want to talk to her," he said.

Even though Larry knew any words would ring pretty hollow at this dark moment, he went forward undeterred, hoping some key phrase would replay itself in Elizabeth's ear when she was calm enough to think clearly. I listened quietly on the extension as she cried and shared her pain. Then Larry offered a tender, loving viewpoint.

"I know you don't want to hear this now, but let's keep things in perspective," he said gently. "Sure, it hurts and you're disappointed, but we'll get through this. Let's all take a deep breath and give it a little time. I know you, Elizabeth, and you're the kind of person who won't let this keep you down. At the moment, it seems like this is absolutely the end of the world, but it's not. There will be another tryout next year, and the fact is, you did your best. No one can ask for anything more than that, and we're both very proud of you for trying out. We love you dearly, Elizabeth, and nothing will ever change that."

But it is the end of the world. This was my only chance. From now on, my social life is over. Now I'll never be one of the popular girls. And worse, Mandy won't have time for me because she'll be at cheerleading practice—I won't have any friends at the new big school. I'm worthless and will never get anything! My dad isn't even here to give me one of his special hugs. He's probably so disappointed in me.

I didn't know how Elizabeth felt, but after hearing Larry's take on the situation, I was inspired. *He's absolutely right!* I said to myself, finally coming out of my own numbed stupor. *I wish I'd thought of saying such wise words!* I charged up the stairs, determined to pick up where Larry left off. I was tempted to give Elizabeth a hug whether she wanted one or not. I knew *I* sure could use one!

I knocked on the door and opened it a bit. "Elizabeth, I was just thinking," I began as I came into her room. "There have been many times in my own life when a door has closed in my face, but God has always opened a window."

Momentarily, she stopped glaring at me and even seemed mildly interested, so I pressed on. "I just thought of a window of opportunity for you. You like to keep busy during summer break, so why not take diving lessons?"

"What are you talking about, Kali? Who's interested in diving?" she protested. "That's a dumb idea."

"Maybe it is, but hear me out. Gymnastics skills can easily transfer into diving skills. And diving will sharpen your body awareness and help you in the cheerleading tryouts next year," I concluded.

Diving—how lame! It isn't even a real sport and definitely won't help me make cheerleader, let alone become part of the "in" crowd. Kali has the dumbest ideas!

"Kali, I don't want to hear about diving. Get out of my room!"

Dodging a hurling pillow, I sheepishly retreated and turned to my most reliable source of reassurance: prayer. "Lord, I have done my best here, and it's been a pitiful mess. Please send some comfort her way and either inspire my words or help me keep my mouth shut. Diving—what was I thinking?" I spewed out my embarrassment and ineptness in one long breath.

"Give it time," came the Wisdom. "Be still and trust."

Slightly calmer, I resisted the temptation to beat myself up for not performing my motherly duty perfectly. I replayed my mental tapes, searching for a "Jodi tip." *Okay, I can't fix this, and our conflicts often involve tone or timing. My tone was good, but I didn't allow time for Elizabeth to work through the sadness before offering my creative thoughts about turning her lemons into lemonade.* "In quietness and rest will be your strength," I said aloud. "Don't just *do* something; *sit* there!"

I backed off. I offered no more advice and allowed Elizabeth to work through this disappointment her own way. A few months later she approached me, waving the recreation center's summer schedule. "Hey, look what came in the mail!" she exclaimed.

Elizabeth always liked to check out the classes offered during summer break, and I could see she had already filled in the enrollment form. I smiled, remembering the time she invited me to take a puff-paint T-shirt-decorating class with her. The fact that I am craft impaired didn't bother her, and for once my perfectionism didn't prevent me from giving something new a go.

I peered over her shoulder to see what she had selected this time, but I was not at all disappointed when my name was missing from the enrollment form. She had circled only one class: diving. I was ecstatic to see her emotionally moving on and applying her considerable talent in a new direction. So often she discarded my suggestions simply because *I* was the one offering the idea; it was one more way she had discovered to cast me aside as a know-nothing plague on her life. Yet this time she had actually moved forward, and I was thrilled by her affirmation. My idea was not lame; it was simply poorly timed. At least it was progress!

From the moment she mounted the diving board, Elizabeth flew through the air with the grace of a swallow and the power of an eagle. When her first meet ended, there stood Elizabeth smiling confidently and extending her hand to receive the first-place ribbon. Joyful tears came to my eyes as I snapped her picture. *Our gravity dancer was born to fly—one way or another!*

That meet was the beginning of a stunning five-year diving career that included many awards. Elizabeth reached the finals in the Texas State High School Championships, earned all-state honors, and eventually qualified to dive in the Junior Olympics Zone competition that featured the top one hundred female divers in America (age fourteen through sixteen). The joys we shared in the process never would have been realized had Elizabeth been chosen cheerleader as she had hoped.

But stellar as her diving accomplishments were, Elizabeth never had a burning passion for the sport. Sure, she loved winning medals and ribbons for diving, but her star was hitched to cheerleading, and nothing would deter her from that dream for long.

Between diving meets, Elizabeth diligently practiced her cheers and tumbling in preparation for the tenth-grade cheerleading tryouts. My anxiety mounted, and I longed to steel her against an emotional crash if things did not turn out well this time.

Unfortunately, whenever I tried to show empathy by relating a similar personal experience, Elizabeth always discounted my example as irrelevant. I decided to give it one more try and share a specific time that God had worked my disillusionments together for good.

"Your desire to be a cheerleader reminds me of my dream early in my business career," I said, anticipating an emotional slap. *Hmmm, no eye rolling yet. Keep going.* "I tried very hard to find a job in public relations when I graduated from college since that was my major, but

I could only find part-time work. Finally, I grew so discouraged that I went to an employment agency."

Elizabeth closed her book and looked up with interest.

Wonder where this is going.

"I filled out the questionnaire, and Joan, the owner of the agency, invited me into her office. She looked at my résumé and asked if I'd ever considered sales. Parroting back to her my public-relations professor's opinion, I explained that sales was *not* public relations and that I would be wasting my education.

"So Joan did a likes/dislikes assessment based on my previous jobs and then showed me in black and white why I would excel in a sales position. 'You just need a highly reputable corporation with a great training department,' Joan told me. She ultimately placed me in a wonderful sales job with a blue-chip company. I was amazed that almost against my will, Joan had managed to lead me onto a path that suited me perfectly. It was as if she knew me better than I knew myself!"

"And the point would be?" Elizabeth asked, not seeing a parallel with cheerleading at all.

"Well, three years later, I decided to change companies. I stopped by to see if Joan could help me with my next career move, but her office was no longer there and a printing company now occupied the space. I figured Joan must have moved, so I went to the phone book, but her agency was no longer listed. I even went to a competing firm and asked if their rival had gone out of business, but they claimed never to have heard of Joan's company. It was as if Joan never had existed," I explained.

Elizabeth's eyes were as big as dinner plates and firmly fixed on me.

"The whole thing was very strange," I concluded. "It was almost as though Joan were divinely placed in my path like a guiding angel of some sort sent to help me find my way."

I waited for Elizabeth to discount the whole thing, but she just sat there as if deep in thought.

"Wow, God really does work in your life. That's amazing!" she said in full faith.

Okay, go for the close. "So you see, honey, even though I was disappointed and felt like a failure at public relations, God guided me into an arena where I could be not only successful but also fulfilled and happy. I just had to be willing to trust. I learned that when He closed a door, I should let go of the handle and look for the open window. I know you are going to do your very best tomorrow, and I truly believe you will come out on top this time. But if things don't work that way, I hope you will trust that God has something even better in mind for you. Either way, you win."

Elizabeth's reaction was hard to decode. She simply smiled a wry smile and headed for the loft to practice her cheers.

Even though I don't know what she's talking about in a business sense, it's pretty cool what she said about God's plan. Maybe God really does have something in mind for me—but I hope it's cheerleading! Hmmm, maybe Kali cares about me after all. I finally feel as if she can relate to what I'm going through.

In the midst of tryout turmoil, I had achieved inner harmony and hoped the same for Elizabeth. I had offered what I could; now I must *do* what I recommended: trust God with the outcome. And order the daisies.

If Only I Had Known . . .
- Timing is just as important as tone. There is a time to share and a time to keep silent.
- Even when children appear to be rejecting your love and advice, most of the time, they *are* listening.

What I Would Have Done Differently

I always had a hard time remembering not to take Elizabeth's rejection personally. She usually acted as if my caring for her didn't matter. In the long run, I've learned that every little offering of love made a difference in her life. Sure, it annoyed her! But she grew to realize that I really did care about her. I could have made things easier on myself by refusing to take her insults personally and remembering that although she might reject my bumbling attempts at a real relationship, I never was wrong to offer them.

I'm so glad I opened up and shared my personal experience and ideas with Elizabeth. However, I really beat myself up when I did it wrong—offering the wrong advice or having bad timing. I might not have been so miserable if I'd offered myself some of the grace that God lavishes upon us constantly. It would have been nice to be reminded that I was responsible only for doing my best and that I could trust God with the outcome.

Reflecting on Your Own Family
- Can you think of instances when your tone and your words were right but your timing was off?
- How can we know when our timing is right and when it's better to wait?
- Think back to some times you thought your stepchildren weren't listening but it later became clear that they *were*. What does this do for your parenting enthusiasm?
- How difficult is it for you to trust God with the outcome in tough parenting situations? What could you do to make it easier?

✳ Chapter Nine ✳

Stepping Up to the Challenge

Childhood is a time of rapid changes. Between the ages of twelve and seventeen, a parent can age thirty years.
—SAM LEVENSON

Despite the beautiful, isolated bonding moments, our bickering continued. I tried to be at peace with the fact that Elizabeth's love revealed itself to me as surprise occurrences rather than a sustained emotion, but after seven years of stepmothering, I was weary, impatient, and eager for extended periods of peace. And just as my dream of consistent harmony with Elizabeth seemed as far off as the peaks of Everest, her fondest dream came true.

"Yes! I finally made cheerleader! I can't wait to get my uniform!" she gushed with glee the day the list was posted.

But soon I discovered that in Texas, cheerleading was a joint commitment and the joyous result of Elizabeth's tryout would have a far-reaching and time-gobbling impact on *my* life too. Her dream was about to become my nightmare.

My mouth gaped open at our first mothers' meeting when I learned of my "duties." I was to make a personal appearance with cameras flashing and video cameras rolling at every football, basketball, soccer, wrestling, volleyball, and women's sporting event. I would proudly display Elizabeth's photo in a humongous button on my shoulder (to properly identify me as a cheerleader mom). It wasn't that these requirements were so bad; it was the militaristic way in which they were communicated that got my hackles up. The feeling was that if you're a *good* mother, you'll do all of *these* things.

I had anticipated much of my involvement in Elizabeth's cheerleading career, but I soon found myself paraphrasing a familiar prayer — "Lord, please forgive me for my debts and help me forgive my debtors" — for the cheerleading experience was one debt after another.

The other mothers seemed delighted to leap headfirst into a variety of fund-raisers to help finance the endless array of bows, bags, uniforms, water jugs, and various other "necessary" items that would all bear the school's stallion logo or a little pair of horseshoes. Later came cheerleading camps and competitions, which involved hotel accommodations, meals, and special spirit paraphernalia to keep the girls happy and motivated. Our shared grand experience would climax with the year-end cheerleading banquet, which required a hefty budget for food, flowers, slide shows, and evening gowns.

The fund-raisers were established so that we could share the joy *and* expense of cheerleading with friends and neighbors by granting them an opportunity to purchase baked goods, candy, pansies, poinsettias, and our garage-sale items at highly inflated prices. Of course, any actual *selling* became a mother's duty because the girls were too busy practicing their cheerleading skills to raise funds themselves (except for an occasional car wash).

However, hitting up friends and relatives for money was not my idea of fair play. "No problem," the cheerleader mother superior assured me. "If you don't like fund-raisers, just shell the money out of pocket. Your choice."

Scaling down the cheerleading activities to allow the girls time to raise their own funds simply was not an option. Struggle as I did to understand the philosophy, after having my hand slapped, I resolutely pitched in to contribute my fair share. But no matter what I did, two things were crystal clear: The whole business was critical to Elizabeth, and my efforts were never enough. Her continual criticism only made me less enthusiastic.

All these plans the moms have are so cool! Why can't Kali just fit in with them? Doesn't she understand how important it is to me? I've always wanted to have a "cheerleader mom." I mean, it's part of the whole package when you make the squad. Once again, Kali's just trying to make my experience miserable. The other moms get along and have fun decorating our lockers and making us goodies. Kali doesn't even try.

I thought I was doing what was required, but apparently my ambivalence showed through my actions. Elizabeth picked up on it, and without my wholehearted enthusiasm, she didn't feel supported or like we were a team. It would be a couple more years before I was able to fully "let it go" and embrace my role in cheerleading. But at the time, I was doing my best, and as the tenth-grade cheerleading year drew to a close, we all prepared for the next round of cheerleader tryouts. These would be even more difficult than before, with much stiffer competition. As I watched Elizabeth prepare, my admiration grew in proportion to her effort. She knocked herself out perfecting cheers until *I* was doing them in *my* sleep.

When I arrived at the school to pick her up after the first day's tryouts, I could tell from a distance that Elizabeth's spirit was downcast, but this time I didn't head into the minefield alone or unprepared. *Lord, please give me the right words*, I prayed as I waited, and a verse came to mind: "Let your speech always be with grace, as though seasoned with salt, so that you will know how you should respond to each person" (Colossians 4:6). I thought about what the verse said and asked that my own conversation would be so blessed. *Give me wisdom to avoid another blunder, and put in my mouth the words a "real" mom would say.*

"I stunk!" came the cry that interrupted my prayer. As soon as the car door slammed behind her, Elizabeth's tears began to flow. We were halfway home before I could gather the details. She wouldn't find out if she'd made the cut until the following day after school. "I completely forgot some of the motions, and my muscles were so sore from all the practicing that my kicks were really low," Elizabeth lamented.

I allowed her to let most of the steam out of her kettle, and then we both cried some gentle tears of disappointment. Finally I summoned my courage and said in truthful reassurance, "Honey, you may not have given your best performance, but I'm fairly confident that you did *not* stink. It's still possible that you made the short list anyway, and you might get another shot tomorrow. The worst thing you can do is get down on yourself tonight."

I paused and waited for her to yell that she hated me and that I was stupid. She sat quietly sniffling, so I kept going. "I've seen how your eyes light up when you perform. Even if you missed a few steps, I'm sure the judges could see that light too. Some girls may have the steps but not the heart." *Whew! She didn't spit out a single word of rejection.*

Elizabeth wiped her eyes, heaved a deep sigh, and asked sweetly, "Do you think you could tell me that same stuff tomorrow before I go in there?"

"Sure," I replied, delighted that she had accepted my encouragement. One of my greatest fears as her stepmother was that this child would reject God if for no reason other than because I loved Him and she hated me. I decided to risk it anyway and offer the one thing that I knew would help: "We can even pray together about it if you want," I concluded, holding my breath.

Wow, sometimes I feel like she really cares about me.

"Okay. Do you think we could go to Wendy's tonight and talk some more about the next tryout?"

I wanted to do a double backflip. "Yeah, Wendy's sounds great," I replied, remembering the day long ago when she peered over her Frosty and asked if she could call me Mother. Though she ultimately retracted that offer, this night as we munched, chatted, and strategized, I realized she was not arguing, rolling her eyes, or changing the subject. We treated each other with mutual respect.

The next day, I fulfilled my promise to encourage her and pray for her. We held hands, bowed our heads in the parking lot, and asked for heavenly help. I carefully avoided the prayer I knew she wanted—I never asked that she'd make the squad, only that God would enable her to do her very best.

The next afternoon, I sat nervously in the car, snapping my eyes to attention each time the gym doors opened. I watched joy and pain pour from the building on the faces of other girls and dreaded the night ahead if Elizabeth's news was sad.

How thrilling it was to see Elizabeth explode through the doors with a smile. "I did it!" she squealed as she bounded up to the car.

Thank You, I silently prayed.

"I couldn't focus on school at all," Elizabeth panted, trying to catch her breath from all the excitement. "None of us could. Everyone was crazy with anticipation of 'the list' being posted at the end of the day. As soon as the final bell rang, I ran as fast as I could to see if my tryout number was posted on the wall. I found my number right away and got hugged by all my friends and new teammates. It was sad and creepy walking past all the other girls who didn't make it. They were all crying so hard, and their mothers looked so sad standing there holding balloons and flowers.

"There's one bad thing," Elizabeth confided. "Mandy didn't make it. I can't believe it, Kali. Not only is she a great cheerleader, she's the one who talked me into trying out in the first place. We've been friends since sixth grade, and I'm afraid she might blame me for taking her spot."

Elizabeth teared up thinking about Mandy, and I blinked back a few tears myself. Mandy had spent many sleepovers in our home, and I was quite fond of her. I hoped the girls' special relationship would not be marred by this development, so we talked about how to handle their friendship moving forward. We reviewed the most helpful things friends had said and done when Elizabeth didn't make the cut, and then we rode in silence awhile.

"Maybe this is one of those times that God is using something bad in my life to help somebody else," Elizabeth observed.

The tenderness between us was palpable. With Larry in Austin during these significant highs and lows, Elizabeth was relying on my wisdom and support more and more. I was amazed and grateful that the hardship Larry's job change appeared to present had actually birthed closeness for me with Elizabeth. *Just one more bad thing that God has worked together for good,* I thought with a smile. But as I said before, sublime tenderness between us was usually followed by sharp pain.

Soon it was time for summer cheerleading camp, and the excitement of the cheerleaders was exceeded only by the exuberance of their mothers. Much as I hated my own attitude, I found myself back in that unwelcome place of wondering why the mothers were putting so much effort into the students' high school experience.

I can't wait for cheerleading camp! It's gonna be so much fun! Plus, I can get away from Kali for awhile. I hope I make a bunch of new friends on the squad. I don't really know most of them that well. I've heard that the moms sneak into our dorm rooms while we're practicing and put up cool decorations and leave us surprises and gifts with Wildcats painted on them and stuff. What a neat reward for working so hard all day.

My camp experience began with a forty-five-minute drive to the university campus in Denton, followed by some heavy lifting. We lugged a mountain of cheer-related belongings, bedding, fans, and snacks into the college dorm room where the girls would be sleeping (a relative term).

The cheerleading moms had determined that the dorm food (which we'd already paid for as part of the camp tuition) would not be suitable. Our precious ones would need home-cooked meals, which we would take turns delivering, and the delivery would be no problem because any "good" mom would be back to the campsite each evening to applaud and videotape what her darling had learned each day.

At the sign-up meeting for our camp duties, I quickly marked my name down for taco shells, figuring anything involving real cooking was best left to the "professionals." Besides, I was under a publisher's deadline for my first book, so I really did not welcome the additional pressure of cooking detail. But because all I had to do was buy the shells and deliver them, I was confident I could handle the task. I went right out and purchased a large quantity of taco shells at the local club store.

But a few days before camp started, I got a call from a concerned mother: "Kali, I was shopping today at the specialty store, and the owner said that our taco shells had not been ordered. Is there a problem?"

Specialty store? "No, there's no problem. I've had the taco shells for days. I got them at Sam's."

"Sam's? No, you were supposed to buy special shells. We're making taco salad, not tacos. We need those nice, large tortilla bowls—not shells," she explained.

"Gosh, I'm sorry. I didn't see anything on the sheet about bowls. I'm on a book deadline and *really* don't have time to drive across town for those bowls. Can we use the shells I already have?"

"Well, we would *prefer* the bowls!" she said, followed by a curt goodbye.

I'm not going to let these mothers-in-overdrive intimidate me. The girls can just eat a taco rather than a taco salad this once, I decided. *My shells will just have to do.* I hoped the whole thing would blow over and be forgotten by camp time.

Soon camp day arrived, and after driving to and from Denton to drop off Elizabeth, I turned back around to make an evening appearance. *I'll bet Elizabeth will be pleased that I made the extra effort tonight. With this big zoom lens, maybe I'll even get some photos good enough to appear in the banquet slide show. Elizabeth always complains that because I don't take enough pictures, she doesn't get in the slide shows as much as some of the other girls.*

I secretly hoped to earn points with my daughter *and* with the "mom squad." When I arrived, many of the girls seemed really glad to see me. They all smiled and posed sweetly for the camera—all except one. Not only did Elizabeth fail to appreciate my extra effort, she totally ignored me! She looked away from the camera every time I tried to snap a shot, and during breaks in activity, she ran off with her friends without even saying a quick hello.

Some of the other cheerleaders came up to tell me a little about their day. But not Elizabeth. And when the festivities were over for the evening, she didn't even say goodbye. She just ran off with the group, leaving me standing in the grass, embarrassed and feeling foolish.

I was so hurt, I cried all the way home. That night when Larry called from Austin, I let him have an earful of my pain. "That's it, Larry. I've bent over backward to support that girl, and I will *not* be treated this way. I'll pick her up on Saturday, but until then, I won't drive an hour and a half to be ignored. From now on, I go to her activities for you and with you, but never again for just her!"

Larry listened and tried to comfort me long-distance. Then before saying good night, he added, "Oh, honey, just one more thing. Don't do it for me or for Elizabeth—do it for yourself. I may not be around forever. The day might come when she's all you've got."

I sat silently after we hung up. What he said was true and never had dawned on me. Both of my parents were dead. I was an only child, and so was Elizabeth. If Larry vanished from our lives, we would both be alone and lonely—except for each other. We were meant to be a blessing to one another.

Nevertheless, if Elizabeth didn't *want* me, I could not stand to show up in her life and be mistreated and ignored (particularly now while I was in hot water with the moms over the taco shells). I figured no one would be talking to me and no one cared if I showed up or not. Even though I was haunted each day by Larry's words, I always came to the same decision: *Why bother? She allows me to come close only so she can slap my face. I'm tired of having my heart jerked around on her imaginary chain. Love is not supposed to be a matter of convenience!*

The final camp day arrived, and I knew that the squads would be into heavy competition. I was upset at not being there to see Elizabeth perform. It was the first time I had missed a competition, but I had a point to make, so I stayed home until the time came to pick her up.

When I finally did arrive, the other mothers were seated in the arena where the competition had taken place. They chatted excitedly about the outcome, and I received a cool reception. I felt awkward and figured the taco gossip had spread to mark me as unfit for their inner circle. But one mother (who apparently didn't care about the shells) rushed over exclaiming, "You missed it! Elizabeth got All-American! Do you know what an honor that is and how few girls ever make it? We're all so proud of her. It was so exciting. The squad did great too. We got top team!"

I can't believe I got All-American honors and Kali missed the whole thing! Of course, she comes on the first night, when we aren't even doing anything, but doesn't bother to show up at the big awards presentation. The worst part is that she didn't get pictures or video to show my dad. I felt like such a geek being the only girl there without her mother cheering like crazy. Kali has some nerve!

My emotions were so tangled up. I was sick about missing Elizabeth's award-winning performance. I would not have it on tape, so she and Larry would be furious. It was a moment that could never be recaptured. *Maybe one of the mothers got at least a photo.*

Elizabeth and I kept our distance from one another and didn't say more than a quick hi before walking in silence to the dorm to retrieve her belongings. The silence continued all the way home, and the air was so hostile that you could smell the tension between us. I was waiting for an apology, and apparently she was too. I'd come too far to start gushing praise and acting as though nothing had happened, so I rode in silence, determined to wait her out.

When we got home, I helped Elizabeth carry a few things in from the car, but I left them on the stairs for her to take to her room. I went to my office and fiddled with paperwork while a lot of door slamming and bad language emanated from Elizabeth's room. I kept still, prayed, and shuffled papers.

Finally, after failing to engage me with doors and muffled accusations, Elizabeth came into my office for a direct confrontation. She began by calling me a few names and concluded by screaming, "You don't even care that I made All-American! How do you think it makes me feel when you don't even bother to show up? I was the only girl there without her mother. You don't have any idea how to be a mother!"

I wheeled around in my swivel chair, burst into tears, and for the first time let my hurt feelings fly openly. "And you are nothing like a real daughter! How dare you tell me I don't care about your making All-American. I've supported everything you've ever done: gymnastics, diving, *and* cheerleading. Don't you think it hurt me to miss seeing you receive your All-American award? Do you think I drove all the way to Denton that first night just to practice my photo techniques? You wouldn't even speak to me. How do you think that made *me* feel? It's always about *your* feelings, Elizabeth. Well, *I* have feelings too, and you've been stomping all over them for years. So unless you can learn to treat me decently when I come to support you, don't look for me in the bleachers."

Amazingly, she ran into my arms. We bawled like babies.

"I'm so sorry, Kali. I don't know why I ignored you. The other girls are always saying I'm lucky to have a stepmom who supports me so much. Some real moms don't even come to as much stuff as you do. I really do want you to be there and watch me cheer. I want you to be proud of me," Elizabeth wailed.

"I'm sorry too, honey," I wailed right back. "I'm *so* proud of you. I just get my feelings hurt when you act like you don't care about me or if I'm there to watch or if I'm even in your life at all. Let's start over and try a little harder, okay?" I sniffed.

Although this would not be our last disagreement, we had reached higher ground, and the air was clearer between us after our mutual apology. Waiting for an enduring bond to materialize with my daughter was a little like watching for a century plant to burst into bloom (it happens only once every hundred years), but I was consoled by the notion that if it ever happened, our blossom would be a stunning standout in our desert landscape.

And it was apparent that God was breathing a cooler breeze across the wasteland of our hearts. We both got a refreshing glimpse of a promise in the midst of being fulfilled. God answered my most fervent prayer and granted me the "feeling" the *real* mothers know.

He calls it "love."

If Only I Had Known . . .

- Sometimes the most valuable gift you can give a child is to go along with *her* agenda and make her top priority *your* top priority.
- It's not unusual—and not unique to stepfamilies—for teenagers to inexplicably give or withhold their love at the most unexpected moments.

What I Would Have Done Differently

When cheerleading began, I wish it had occurred to me what a profound impact it might have had if I'd simply let go of all my objections and charged full speed ahead as the awesome cheerleader mom Elizabeth wanted. I was living up to my requirements physically, but in my heart I was resentful of having to do things I really didn't agree with. I should have realized that Elizabeth would pick up on this. It didn't occur to me that being a cheerleader mom was my opportunity for the heart connection I'd been wanting with Elizabeth all along.

Even though I'd learned so much by talking with other mothers, I still attributed Elizabeth's changeable nature to our stepfamily situation. It had hurt my feelings so much when she ignored me at cheerleading camp, yet it didn't occur to me that any child might have done this, not just a stepchild. It still could have happened—and wouldn't have hurt any less—had I been Elizabeth's natural mother. In hindsight, would I still have responded by refusing to attend camp the rest of the week? Probably! It was a boundary that needed to be set. Our relationship was stronger when I refused to be treated badly.

Reflecting on Your Own Family

- Think of a child-related event that required your full participation and enthusiasm. How easy or difficult was it for you to give up your own agenda and go with the flow?

- Do you blame most of your difficult parenting moments on the "stepfamily" situation? How would your attitude change if you were to discover that your problems are common to all types of families?
- In hindsight, have you made any major decisions regarding your children that you now regret? How would you change those decisions if you could?
- What are some ways you can keep your eyes open to opportunities for making deeper connections with your stepchildren?

✳ Chapter Ten ✳

Stepping Out in Faith

Hear, my son, your father's instruction
And do not forsake your mother's teaching;
Indeed, they are a graceful wreath to your head
And ornaments about your neck.
—Proverbs 1:8-9

The flower of respect between us that began to bud during the cheer-camp fiasco bloomed into full flower before Elizabeth's high school graduation. It seemed God was preparing our child for university life by changing her from an unappreciative, name-calling pillar of criticism into a frequently grateful daughter. At the same time, He reshaped me from a cynical, taco-bowl-bashing Judge Judy into a "too-bad-it's-over-so-soon," sentimental mom. Buoyed by Elizabeth's more appreciative attitude, I had finally leaped aboard the cheerleader moms' bandwagon, and to my amazement, I thoroughly enjoyed the ride. What divine metamorphosis!

Perhaps it was angst over the changes ahead, however, that prompted Elizabeth's attitude problems to flare up during the final month before college. As the time drew near, even Larry was muttering under his breath, "I think it's time for her to be on her own."

For so many years, I'd dreamed of the moment when Elizabeth would head off to college. When I thought about it (which was usually when ducking a verbal assault), my only projected emotion was jubilation. During our more difficult times, I even comforted myself with a countdown to college: "Only nine more years," and then, "Only five more years," and finally, "Only one more week!"

I often grew silent in the presence of mothers who seemed on the verge of a breakdown at the mention of graduation day. Looking into a tearstained face, I could never admit that deep down I was eager to switch my focus from child rearing to nuptial harmony. Those heartbroken women can't possibly understand why I dream of Elizabeth living on campus or relate to my longing for bicker-free alone time with Larry. Unlike the way it was for any other mother I knew, the empty nest had always been a welcome thought to me.

My guilt was immense. *Does God "get" mothers who look forward to their kids leaving home?* I wondered. *Does feeling this way mean I have utterly failed at being a mom?* I heard no reply from heaven, but I've since learned it's a common experience for stepmothers. When the parenting road is so long and arduous, it's natural to relish the idea of a reprieve.

But when the time came to watch our girl wing it alone, my perspective changed. I wondered what Elizabeth was feeling. Was she excited and raring to go, or was she apprehensive and nervous about the possibility of free fall? Was she worried about making mistakes? Was she numb and confused like I felt at the moment? I doubted that. Elizabeth seemed to be floating on air.

I listened to her singing her favorite Dixie Chicks song, "Wide Open Spaces," as she packed. I didn't even ask her to lower the volume on the music blaring from her room, knowing that soon our house would be *too* quiet. "She needs wide open spaces, room to make her big mistakes. She needs new faces. . . ."[3] I blinked back a few tears and wondered who those new faces would be and how they would influence my child.

Wow, all summer long I've been singing this song and dying to get out of this house, but now that I'm really leaving, I feel kind of weird. I've been so looking forward to being on my own, yet as much as I hated Dad and Kali nagging me to do things, I don't know how I am going to survive without their structure in my life. What if I can't do everything on my own? I mean, my roommate sure won't be willing to go through what Kali does just to wake me up for class each morning. Man, I must be the soundest sleeper in Texas. What if I oversleep every day for the whole first semester?

I have to admit that it's been kind of nice having someone else do my massive loads of laundry and fix my flat tires! I'm kind of thinking I should have just stayed close by and gone to Southern Methodist University. When I picked Kansas, I was reminiscing about good times in Lawrence and looking forward to being out from under house rules. At the time, I thought being on my own would be totally cool. But Kansas is really far away. Am I ready for all of this responsibility? What if I can't handle it by myself?

Boy, with my stuff out of here, this barely looks like my room anymore. Even though I'm never going to live here again, I hope they don't rush to turn my room into an exercise loft or something. I'd better remind them not to take down my trampoline either. I might want to jump on it next summer—when I come home for a visit. My stomach is feeling kind of upset. Maybe I'll feel better after breakfast. Well, everything is packed. I can't put this off any longer. I better go down and eat something.

I shuffled around the kitchen, rearranging things to release my tension and take my mind off of the approaching moment when I would hug our daughter goodbye. I stared blankly out the window at the garden. Today my ruby-red begonias offered no comfort or whisper of encouragement. I wandered over to the refrigerator and opened the door for no apparent reason. I was gloomy, dazed, even disoriented—

but I certainly wasn't hungry. My emotions were so fragile that I felt almost as though a death had occurred. *I can't believe this time has come so quickly.* I slowly closed the refrigerator door and shook my head in disbelief. How brief our time together had been after all. *Well, the moment has come and you'd better get a grip, old girl. This morning will be hard enough without adding tears to the situation. You'll have plenty of time to cry once she drives off.*

While I poured myself another cup of coffee and paced the house in a zombie-eyed gaze, Larry busied himself in the garage. He was rearranging the contents of Elizabeth's bulging backseat and the trunk of her car for the fourth time. I always figured we'd both head off to Kansas with Elizabeth, help her unpack, and tuck her securely into her college environment like a toddler with her blankie. As things turned out, there was barely enough space in the car for a driver and one passenger. We all agreed that only Larry should accompany Elizabeth. He'd help out with the eight-hour drive to Kansas University and then fly back. But I hadn't counted on this lump in my throat and the prospect of an entire weekend alone with no one to help me process my pain. *What am I going to do with all of these feelings?*

I was comforted only slightly by the fact that the following weekend, Larry and I would head back to Kansas for my high school reunion. I was thankful that providential timing would enable me to have a reunion with Elizabeth as well. I felt somewhat cheated at not being able to witness the moment her pretty new bedspread unfurled or see the mountain of colorful new pillows adorning her dorm room bed. I wanted to see her fluffy, yellow towels arranged on the towel bar, and her toothbrush sitting in its stand. Oh, and I would like to check out that cafeteria more closely and examine the laundry room arrangement more fully than I had when we toured campus earlier. At the base of it all, I longed to observe our daughter moving across the backdrop of her new grown-up life—to see the initial moments of her solo flight for myself and *know* that she would soar.

I went for a tissue, and gazed into the mirror. *Who is this strange woman who has inhabited my skin? You never counted on being left behind when Elizabeth left for school, did you? Elizabeth is probably thrilled to have a father-daughter college experience without you tagging along. Serves you right for all the negative things you have been thinking about her for so long.* "It wasn't supposed to feel like this," I told my reflection.

I fought to chase away the huge tears threatening to roll down my cheeks. I'd always imagined this off-to-college scene very differently than it was playing out in real life. My imaginary movie enactment went more like this:

✳

We would drive to KU and commence the grand move into the dorm. I would offer to make Elizabeth's bed while she and Larry unloaded the rest of the car. Elizabeth would walk in the door with an armful of clothes, see her bed, throw a hissy fit, and scream, "Kali, you did it all wrong!"

With the move-in complete, we would meet her roommate and the kids across the hall. We would stand at her door, uncomfortably shuffle our feet, and invite Elizabeth for a final family dinner. She would decline, Larry would feel rejected, and we would drive back to Dallas in a blue funk.

For the first hundred miles, Larry would cry while I consoled. Then he would verbally relive every cute thing Elizabeth had done since her birth. Eventually, he would get to the part where I entered their lives and relive each gymnastics meet, diving competition, cheerleading moment, and academic accomplishment.

The movie dialogue would soon evolve into our speculations about Elizabeth's exciting college life. All of this would take about four hours of the eight-hour drive back to Dallas, with tears flowing at intervals along the way. During the final four hours, Larry would repeat the entire conversation word for word as if it never had taken place. I would say very little but would nod and comfort appropriately and wonder how long it would be before my husband could speak Elizabeth's name without tearing up.

The final scene of the movie would be Elizabeth's college graduation, where Larry ultimately would concede that he likes living in a clean, orderly house and lingering over a satisfying meal at a *real* restaurant. Ah, romance lives!

✳

Yet somewhere during our family journey, I fired my movie-scenario development team and started *enjoying* our daughter. Somehow we had moved from brokenness to blessing, and quite to my surprise, I dreaded the thought of her car pulling out of our driveway.

As Elizabeth bounded down the stairs for breakfast, I struggled to think of something profound to say. On other occasions, her exuberance had left black marks on my walls, and dirty walls had prompted my temper to flare too frequently. I regretted that now. I didn't want her to leave without knowing how much my love for her had grown.

For many reasons, I did not have the courage to express a straightforward "I love you dearly and I will miss you like crazy." I doubted that Elizabeth would accept such a sentiment as heartfelt. The fear of rejection dies hard.

Hmmm, this is the last time I will ever have to eat my breakfast with Kali's workout music blaring through the kitchen speakers. I'll bet the dorm will have all different types of cereal to choose from and bacon—not the health-nut, turkey bacon we have around here, but real bacon like Grandma makes.

She was slipping away. Nine years . . . five years . . . one year to college. Those years are gone now! Self-recrimination poured through my heart like a hard rain flows through a downspout. *Why were we enemies when we could have been friends? Why did we express affection only when Larry was away? Why was love like a competition where someone must lose before someone else could win? Why had it taken years for me to even ask myself such important questions? Was I afraid to love Elizabeth fully because I feared I could not let go when the time came? Why do I allow a fear of rejection to rule in my soul and keep me silent even now?*

Suddenly, as if God's fingers had tickled my funny bone, I felt a nudge in my spirit urging me to try a gentle jest. I knew from past experience that humor is a language Elizabeth and I speak well. I mustered a grin and somehow blurted out, "Well, squirt, my friends were right about one thing."

Squirt? I am certainly not a squirt anymore. I mean, I'm gonna be living on my own now, making my own decisions and doing things for myself. As much as I get embarrassed by her calling me that, it kind of makes me feel good inside—as though she likes me.

"What do you mean? Right about what?" she asked, readjusting her headband and brushing the hair away from her eyes.

"Everyone has been telling me that just about the time I'd start to like you, you'd be leaving home!" I giggled and hugged her shoulders as she sat at the table eating her cereal.

I wanted her to see the truth and the humor behind my words. For so long, we really didn't enjoy each other, but lately we were closer. A deep connection had occurred in my soul that now would make saying goodbye difficult. I wondered if she felt it too.

This is weird. I think she's actually going to miss me! I have to admit, I'm going to miss her too.

Elizabeth responded by carrying on with the joke from her

perspective: "Yeah, right. You and Dad will be so happy to get rid of me that you'll probably head off to Disney World like that empty-nest television commercial." She paused and then concluded with a grin, "I know for sure you won't miss me on laundry day!"

We laughed out loud.

Man, Kali and I have come a long way, now that I look back on it. Ten years ago I wanted to break up the wedding, but now I'm glad I didn't! She really has been trying to be a good mom. Everything might not have been exactly as I would have planned, but I think she honestly tried her best.

We sat grinning and munching our cereal in warm silence. We'd come a long way, baby. Somehow with God's help, I had ceased looking at an empty nest as my saving grace. At some precise moment that I cannot quite recall, I started looking at my daughter through the eyes of grace instead.

Elizabeth used to tell her friends, "I'm going to have to teach Kali how to be a mother." She was right—she did. She taught me that a mother is all about love—love that is kind and patient, not arrogant, jealous, rude, selfish, or, above all, easily provoked. A mother is not too busy to listen, self-involved, or easily discouraged. She keeps trying. A mother's love bears, believes, and hopes.

And above all, a mother never fails to love, even when the love is not returned.

If Only I Had Known . . .

- The child who swore to be my enemy would turn out to be a treasured friend.
- Love never fails—we only fail to love.

What I Would Have Done Differently

We never know how things are going to turn out. We can take things only one day at a time. I had no way of knowing I'd actually be sad when Elizabeth left home, but when that day came, I suddenly felt that I'd wasted so much time fighting with Elizabeth rather than recognizing her as a gift from God—a blessing.

People always tell young parents, "Enjoy your kids—they'll be gone before you know it." I purposely ignored these comments, assuming the well-meaning advice-givers had no idea what I was going through. How could I possibly enjoy this? But now I think they might have known. They knew about the heartache, the disappointments, and the unmet expectations. And they also knew that the moment it was over, there would be an ache in my heart that I couldn't explain. I wish I'd followed the advice and taken more time to enjoy the parenting ride. Somehow I could've found a way. It might have been difficult, but it would have been worth it.

Reflecting on Your Own Family

- How do you envision feeling when your stepchildren leave home?
- Is there a chance you may be wrong?
- In what ways have your stepchildren taught you to be a mother?
- Are there some things you can start doing differently in order to prevent feelings of regret when your kids leave home?

* Chapter Eleven *

One Step Closer to Heaven

*God knows that a mother needs fortitude and courage and
tolerance and flexibility and patience and firmness and
nearly every other brave aspect of the human soul.*
—PHYLLIS McGINLEY

"College is awesome!" Elizabeth exclaimed, describing her freshman year. "This has been the best year of my life. I can't wait for the fall semester!"

Our daughter's first foray into independence was beyond a parent's dearest hope and a coed's wildest delight. Not only did Elizabeth realize her childhood dream of becoming a college cheerleader like her mother, she also pledged Kappa Alpha Theta (her first pick of all the sororities) and had a tremendously exciting social life. Eventually, our coquette also captured the fancy of the football quarterback (with whom she has found true love). All this excitement, and good grades to boot! Yes, our Elizabeth had taken to college life like a birdie to a worm: She ate it right up!

I'm learning how to be successful in school and in my social life! I'm making so many friends, and I've accumulated enough T-shirts from frat parties to clothe a small country!

My dream of a lasting bond with Elizabeth was magically material-izing too. With more time apart, our bickering ceased and the respect that had developed between us before high school graduation blos-somed all the more once she hit the KU campus.

I'm having an absolute blast at school, and my relationship with my parents is better than ever. It seems like practically overnight they have become my friends. I would almost go as far as saying they are cool. Maybe absence does make the heart grow fonder!

It seemed to me that God had prepared my stepdaughter for university life by granting her an extra dose of self-confidence as she said goodbye to high school days. The rejection Elizabeth experienced at her first cheerleading tryout seemed to have been forever erased by the three years of cheering euphoria that had followed. In high school, she had competed as part of an all-star squad that won a national championship, been named All-American several times, and been hired for a National Cheerleading Association staff position. Then to put the icing on the pom-poms of her senior year, she had been voted Cheerleader of the Year by her peers.

My attitude as collegiate mom matured from my early high school perspective too. I was *eager* to march in lockstep with the Theta moms (or at least keep up as enthusiastically as possible from Texas!). And we had approached KU cheerleading tryouts as a team—we'd held hands and prayed for God's blessing. It seemed to me that almost from the moment she unpacked her clothes and hung them in the closet at Naismith Hall, Elizabeth and I were on the same wavelength.

Elizabeth called several times a week just to talk (thank heaven for free weekend-minutes). Frequently I would awaken at 2 AM to a cheery voice saying things like, "You should see this snowfall! Guess what happened today! Oh my gosh, I've got to tell you about the cool frat party." And her calls always ended with "I love you, bye!" I didn't even mind being aroused from a sound sleep by the sound of her voice anymore. When I went up for Theta Moms' Weekend, she didn't even want me to stay in the hotel like the other mothers but instead invited me to stay at the Theta house.

Wow, Kali has somehow turned into a fun older sister instead of the wicked witch she used to be. My friends really like her, and I actually do too. Why did I dislike her so much growing up?

Best of all, Elizabeth was no longer embarrassed by me. She even seemed delighted to introduce me to her college friends, and I detected a hint of pride when she said, "This is my mom!" And when one of the basketball players told us how much we looked alike, we spontaneously looked into each other's eyes, giggled, and said, "Gee, thanks!" And we meant it.

Gosh, some of the "big men on campus" are actually giving my mom a look. Hanging out with her is so much fun!

Things were pretty groovy in Dallas too as Larry and I returned to lovebird land. With a little breathing space in the nest and a happy daughter on campus, our three-way love affair was just about as good as it gets. Now the harmony Larry craved seemed more like our family motto than like a pipe dream.

When the semester ended in May, Elizabeth settled back into our home for the summer. Larry and I were excited to have her buzzing around the house, and we enjoyed the happy sound of young voices coming and going (even if it was at all hours of the night). She was home only a short time before dashing off to summer cheerleading camp, but thankfully she returned by Father's Day.

I was delighted to see she had learned some practical things while away at school—like cooking! One day she said, "Hey, I have a neat new recipe to try. How about if I make lunch?"

College sure is having a great effect on her. Not only is Elizabeth a joy to be with but she's turned into a gourmet chef! (A wonderful bonus for me, the cooking-impaired mom.)

But when lunch was served and I sat down to a delicious chicken and pasta dish, Elizabeth sat down to a plate of steaming broccoli with fat-free spray butter and soy sauce.

"Is that all you're eating?" I asked, puzzled. "I thought you were looking forward to sampling this new recipe yourself."

"Nah, I just wanted to make it. I'm not really hungry. Is it good?" she asked.

"Delish!" I exclaimed as I downed another bite of pasta. We chatted merrily about Zach (the man of her dreams, who was back in Kansas doing two-a-day football practices most of the summer) and caught up on the day-to-day details of life. I was perplexed by her broccoli "entrée" but shrugged it off, just as I did her announcement about no more partying for the summer.

"I want to eat healthy and get in shape instead," she explained.

This will be a short-lived resolution, I thought. *She's already in shape, and she's always kept socializing a top priority.*

Then our happy train smashed into the side of a mountain that no one saw on the horizon. Elizabeth's lifestyle drastically changed after camp. Before camp, she had been jogging daily with Larry, who was delighted by their father/daughter bonding. But after camp, she wanted to run alone, and exercise became an obsession. Previously a night person, Elizabeth now would get up early and go for long morning runs, do stomach crunches in front of the TV in the afternoon, and close each day with another run.

Because she had been involved in heavy physical activity for years, I wasn't unduly alarmed by the stepped-up exercise routine. *She's accustomed to a hectic pace at KU, and she's bored here. She's probably just trying to keep busy.*

I was wrong. Soon she was not going out with friends *at all*. Even though she had scads of messages from friends who were home for the summer and wanted to hang out, she never returned their calls. Then she signed up for a free summer membership at a nearby sports club and made workouts her only social activity. *What's happening to our social butterfly?* I wondered.

My friends here aren't the same as they used to be. We've all gone to separate schools, and we're different now. We just don't have anything in common anymore. Besides, all social activities involve eating, and I just don't want to deal with that.

All the while, she continued to eat mostly broccoli. When I noticed a bottle of diet pills in her gym bag, I *had* to speak up.

"Are you on some kind of diet?" I asked.

"Yeah, I decided I needed to lose a few pounds and take off that freshman fifteen," Elizabeth explained with a grin.

"Well, I don't think you've got fifteen to lose, squirt," I replied. "What's motivating this?"

"When I didn't get picked for the competitive squad at cheerleading tryouts, I asked the coach what I could do to improve. He said it might help if I lost a few pounds," she explained, "so that's my goal. I love cheering at the games, but I want to compete with the squad too."

"Honey, you don't need to lose any weight. You've got a darling figure. All this broccoli and exercise is getting extreme," I said, sharing my growing concern.

"Back off, Kali. I'm fine," she warned. "My cheering partner graduated, and next year's guys aren't as beefy as Brad was. I have to lose weight so my new partner can lift me for the basket tosses."

Remembering the chasm that developed when my mother tried to exert control over my life after I'd snipped the apron strings, I decided not to widen the gap. *I really don't want to interfere with my eaglet just as she is learning to fly,* I thought, so I backed off but voiced my concern to Larry.

"Have you noticed that Elizabeth is exercising a lot and hiding in her room like a recluse?" I asked. "All she eats is broccoli, and I even saw diet pills in her gym bag. I'm worried she may be developing some kind of eating disorder."

"Yes, I've noticed, and I'm a bit concerned," Larry replied, "but I did talk with Elizabeth, and she assured me she's just trying to get back to what she weighed before going off to college. At least she wants to spend her summer doing something healthy rather than living on a steady diet of late-night partying. She's dedicated her summer to making that competitive squad, and she's focused. We'll keep an eye on her. For now let's take a deep breath and not overreact, okay?"

But I was *not* okay. I remembered Elizabeth's diving coach had questioned me once about her eating habits. At the time, I didn't see any change in them at home, so I dismissed the cautionary red flag then, but now it was flapping in my face.

The rest of the summer was a disaster. The less Elizabeth ate, the more sour her mood. *I'd be crabby too if I nibbled on only raw vegetables,* I thought. Yet I hated to see our closeness start to erode. Our old adversarial patterns were showing signs of returning, and she was even snarling at Larry, as well as at anyone else who crossed her path. She was crawling deeper into her shell.

Why are they being so hard on me? I'm finally getting healthy. Most parents beg their kids to put down the pizza and start exercising. There is an obesity epidemic in this country, for goodness sakes!

By the end of August, Elizabeth had dropped nearly fifteen pounds, but it wasn't fat dropping off; it was fifteen pounds of solid muscle. She didn't have an once of fat on her body even before the diet began. Gymnastics, diving, and cheerleading had produced an amazingly high metabolism and a gorgeous silhouette. But her toned, athletic beauty was fading rapidly.

When August came and it was time for Elizabeth to head back to campus, Larry was so concerned that he made her promise not to lose any more weight. While she verbally agreed, my fears were escalating. I nonchalantly questioned a few friends of mine who had experience with eating disorders, and those conversations produced an all-out panic within. I quickly made our situation a matter of prayer with my special confidantes and prayer partners at church. As fearful as I was for Elizabeth to head for Kansas so far away from our watchful eyes, I knew God was with her.

I could hardly wait for September, when Elizabeth would be back in Dallas for the SMU football game. Ordinarily it would have been a joyful chance to watch Elizabeth cheer and Zach throw touchdown passes, because KU was heavily favored to win. But as an upset unfolded on the field, the upset in my stomach tied me up in knots. I peered through binoculars and spotted her doing backflips on the sidelines. I also saw the pencil-thin arms and emaciated face of our once beautiful girl. I had to fight back tears. Yet I dared not let myself start crying because I feared I might not be able to stop, and we were expecting post-game guests: All of the cheerleaders were coming over for a victory celebration.

We had dolled up the house with festive flowers, balloons, napkins, tablecloths, cups, plates, and utensils all in dear old KU crimson and blue. We also ordered a cookie bouquet with little cookie bears iced in outfits to look like cheerleaders, one for each guy and girl. Elizabeth was delighted by the cookie bouquet but never ate one. And I was dismayed by what she *did* eat: a dab of fruit and three small bites of a grilled chicken breast with no bun. I did *not* serve broccoli.

"I'll take the cookies back with me to school," Elizabeth promised. But I doubted if they would ever be eaten.

Once the kids all piled in the van and headed back to Kansas, I quickly grabbed Larry's arm. "Honey, did you notice how she kept that jacket on all evening?" I asked. "And did you hug her? She's so thin, I could feel every bone in her knobby spine. And her cheeks are all hollowed out!" I exclaimed in horror.

"I noticed, and I reminded her about her promise not to lose any more weight," Larry explained. "I also told her to see a doctor. She said she would make an appointment, so let's not panic. Meanwhile, I'll do some research on the Internet, and then let's see if there's any improvement at the Oklahoma game," he suggested.

I was thankful that Larry was concerned, even if (as was true to his nature) he was not in a panic as I was. So I decided to quit talking and pray silently: *Lord, please send something or someone to stop her. Let her get caught.* I tried to calm my fears with the knowledge that Larry had an ace in the hole: Ann Gabrick. In an effort to calm one of my pleading sessions about Elizabeth's need for counseling, Larry had told me about Ann.

"It was the strangest thing," he explained. "A few years ago I was in Florida and the TV was on in my hotel room. I heard Ann's name and glanced up in time to see Annette's old college roommate being interviewed on national TV. Turns out, Ann is an expert on eating disorders and heads up the unit at Baptist Medical Center in Kansas City. If things get worse, I'll give her a call, but I'd rather give Elizabeth a chance to correct the problem first. This thing may blow over without us dragging Ann into it."

So I bit my nails a while longer until one night the call came. "Mr. Schnieders, this is Dr. Martin. I'm here with Elizabeth, and we have a problem. It seems your daughter's weight has dropped significantly, and I am quite concerned. She is well below the average weight for her height, and this can be very dangerous for her heart, bones, and female organs. I'm going to recommend to the coach that she not be allowed to cheer until her weight is back within a safe range. And I'm afraid your daughter needs more treatment than we can provide at the university clinic."

No sooner had Larry hung up the phone than it was ringing again. "Dad, they're kicking me off the squad. This dumb doctor won't let me cheer until I gain like ten pounds. It's ridiculous; I'm fine."

Why is everyone making such a big deal? I may not be as strong as I used to be, but the guys love stunting with me now, and I get to be on top of the pyramids because I am so light! Anyway, some of the other girls on the squad are skinnier than I am. They still get to cheer.

And so the most terrifying part of our nightmare began.

Larry immediately called Ann Gabrick, and we devoured books on eating disorders. By early November, our daughter was hospitalized with a diagnosis of anorexia nervosa. We were horrified to learn that approximately 20 percent of anorexic victims never recover.

I am so scared and mad and confused. I never have had to go to the hospital before. What will I tell my friends and family and teachers? At least if I had cancer or something, people would feel sorry for me. Nobody will understand.

While in the hospital, Elizabeth continued her schoolwork over the Internet and coped with a barrage of counseling sessions, group therapy, doctor exams, art therapy, and hospital eating rules. Larry and I grappled simultaneously with family counseling, parental support groups, and mountains of insurance forms—and guilt.

We learned that *what* we said, *how* we said it, and *when* we said it would have to be run through a filter of "How will this help or hurt Elizabeth's recovery?" It was the ultimate eggshell walk. Furthermore, our personal eating habits, methods of support, and history of perfectionist tendencies were coming into question as possible culprits that contributed to this problem. We were devastated.

We tried to wrap our minds around baffling recovery concepts: "This is not about eating; it is about control. Most patients feel their life is out of control, and they try to have power over their food intake in order to feel powerful. Unfortunately, they are fooling themselves and are really more out of control than ever. The root cause is usually low self-esteem often combined with perfectionism, but anorexia can be brought on by a trauma from childhood. Only Elizabeth has the key to this lock, and we'll have to wait until she's willing or able to set herself free. The best thing you can do is stick by her, give her all the love and support possible, and wait."

Nothing to do with eating? Low self-esteem? What about the self-confidence she displayed as a competitive diver and cheerleader? If she'd just grab a Frosty and ditch the broccoli, she'd be fine. How can you say that this has nothing to do with eating? Look at her—she's thin as a pipe cleaner! These are just a few thoughts that went through our minds. We heard similar comments from other distraught parents on Family Days (three days a week—our only visiting opportunities). We were universally flabbergasted.

But Larry and I reminded ourselves that this was not about us: it was about our daughter. And eventually it began to sink in that we were literally fighting for her *life*. Somehow we must wrestle Elizabeth away from a lying demon that had snatched her right from under our noses and convinced her she was fat.

We were told from the beginning, "There will be no quick fix. Prepare for one step forward and three steps back. Full recovery may take several years. Furthermore, expect waves of anger and oceans of tears accompanied by despair, blame, and then hopefully healing."

Larry and I held hands as we walked up to sign the visitor sheet, carrying our flowers wrapped in tissue paper. (The girls were not allowed a glass vase, as someone might break it and use the shards to end her life.) We were petrified.

This is the worst thing that's happened in my entire life! It's not fair! There is nothing wrong with me. These girls are sick freaks. I don't belong in this hospital with them. Besides, I have classes, club meetings, and sorority functions that I simply cannot miss. Everyone just wants to make me fat and unhappy.

Thankfully, Larry had retired a few weeks after Elizabeth's hospitalization, so he was able to hop in the car and rush to Kansas City for an extended stay. Meanwhile, I booked a later flight and made a few preparations (like stopping the mail and fulfilling my speaking commitments) before joining him. My time alone in Dallas was excruciating because my mind was always in Kansas. I sent cards and phoned several times a day, hoping to communicate that we were all in this together—as a family.

Sadly, one Sunday Larry had to deal with a harrowing moment alone. He and Elizabeth had been watching television in the family area when the nurse came by to unlock the bathroom (patients are denied at-will access because those with bulimia might try to purge). Mercifully, bulimia was not a part of Elizabeth's diagnosis, but while she was using the restroom, Larry heard a loud, sickening thud from inside the door.

He froze in his chair momentarily and then dashed madly for a nurse. Traumatized by Annette's collapse in a bathroom, my husband was gripped by an unspeakable terror. Fortunately, it was a fainting episode, which is not uncommon with the medication Elizabeth was taking. Larry breathed a sigh of relief. But now it was my turn to face a fear.

Ann Gabrick apparently sensed that Elizabeth needed to feel some sort of "connection" to her mother, so she brought some never-before-seen photos from their college days. Elizabeth called excitedly to tell me the news: "I'm the spitting image of my mom when she was my age! I've been showing all the girls how much we look alike. I can't wait to show you the pictures!" she squealed.

Oh dear, I thought. I knew I had to act pleased as punch to see the photos, but I was not excited about the prospect of hearing the "Annette" stories all over again. *I hope I can pull this off,* I thought, terrified that my jealousy would resurface. To my surprise, from the moment I stepped into that hospital wing of pitiful, precious girls, God melted my heart in a way I never could have anticipated.

Elizabeth headed down the corridor toward us, album in hand. I barely recognized our daughter; her five-foot-seven inches seemed so diminutive in her childlike frame. She looked like a holocaust survivor, and it took every ounce of control I had not to burst into tears.

I sucked it up, and we headed off to see her room. Along the way, she occasionally stopped to show a newfound friend the album. "This is my mom. See how much we look alike!" she exuberantly gushed.

We entered her stark room and arranged the flowers we'd brought in the plastic water pitcher provided by a kind nurse. I smiled when I saw that the encouragement cards I'd sent were proudly displayed on her little dresser top.

"Come see the pictures of Mommy," she said in a little-girl voice. She patted the bed for Larry and me to have a seat. We snuggled as a tight threesome on the small bed while she slowly turned the pages in the album. A miracle unfolded: As I witnessed the joy in our daughter's eyes, a dark door in the recesses of my heart creaked open. My jealousy of Annette simply flew away like a happily released dove. I could not believe it: All jealousy was gone.

Elizabeth's need for her mother's touch was so plainly obvious that even this formerly wicked stepmother could not wish to deny her the pleasure. I looked my former rival in the face (with the aid of yellowing Polaroid film) and for the first time, I felt only love.

Elizabeth was right: She *was* the spitting image of the twenty-year-old girl in the photo. *She needs you now, Annette. Whatever you can offer and however you can give it to her, she needs your touch.* I finally saw Annette and me as allies, co-parents of this mercurial child. I slipped my arm around *our* daughter and drew her head to my shoulder. "She's beautiful," I said.

"Oh, I almost forgot," Elizabeth replied. "Wait till you see this!" She reached for a box underneath the bed and pulled out an afghan. "Ann gave this to me. My mother knitted it for her as a wedding gift. Cool, huh?" she said proudly.

Larry's moist eyes met mine, and I turned to wipe away a tear before Elizabeth could see it. "It's way cool, sweetheart. It's the most beautiful thing I've ever seen," I said. And I meant it.

By divine appointment, God had tenderly placed this blanket

knitted by a mother's loving hands around the shoulders of a child literally starving for her mother's affectionate touch.

"Honey," I pleaded, looking deeply into Elizabeth's eyes and cupping her chin in my hand. "I want you to promise me that every night as you drift off to sleep, you will cover yourself with this blanket and imagine your mother's arms around you. When you are frightened or confused, just wrap yourself in this blanket of your mother's love. Her fingerprints are all over this afghan, and through it she is reaching out from heaven to comfort you. You are *not* alone." Then I reached in my purse and presented Elizabeth with a pretty necklace. It was a small, silver box dangling from a lovely chain. Inside the box was a prayer. "I want you to take this out and read it every day. Let it be your recovery motto," I urged.

Elizabeth unrolled the scroll inside her prayer box and read aloud, "Cast all your anxieties on him, for he cares about you" (1 Peter 5:7, RSV).

This strange woman my dad fell in love with has forgiven the past and stood by my side when I thought I was alone. Even though I've called her every name in the book (and a few more I made up), she stuck it out.

Kali never had any real obligation to do anything for me, but she has somehow changed from an enemy into my most solid rock of support. And now when I truly thought my world had fallen apart, she found just the right words to put it back together. I guess God knew what He was doing, although many times I didn't think so! He didn't just give me a stepmom—He gave me a friend for life.

Several weeks into treatment, Elizabeth ran to greet me on Family Day. She was carrying something she'd made in art therapy. "I hope you like it," she said, handing me an adorable stuffed teddy bear with wings and a halo. My cuddly bear was holding a little box with writing on the top that read, "Truffles from Heaven" (the title of my first book). Inside the box was a smaller box that read, "A truffle of love from Elizabeth." Inside *that* box was a heart made of red pipe cleaners, and underneath it was a blue paper (to represent the sky) and two fluffy cotton balls signifying clouds. I read the words Elizabeth had written for me in glitter: "He will send His angel before you" (Genesis 24:7).

"God sent His angel, all right," I said, kissing her and intentionally leaving my red lip print on her cheek. We hugged and remained for a moment in the embrace, silent and thankful for the gift of each other.

Was I her angel? Was she mine? I had a feeling God intended it to be both ways.

If Only I Had Known . . .
- Parenting doesn't end the day the child leaves for college.
- Making peace with the "real" mom becomes possible when you finally believe *you're* a real mom.

What I Would Have Done Differently
After twelve years of stepparenting, I was finally doing some things right. I was concerned about Elizabeth's health and behavior, but I didn't panic and instead deferred to Larry's wisdom. Without judgment or recrimination, I was there for her when she needed me. I was able to express my genuine love and deep caring for her. God had really been working hard on this formerly wicked stepmother!

What would I have done differently? I certainly wish I could have done something to prevent Elizabeth's anorexia, but whatever part I played in that was long past. All I could do now was stay by her side, support her, and once again trust God for the outcome. That's what I did, and for once I can't think of a thing I'd change.

Reflecting on Your Own Family
- Has your family ever experienced a major life-threatening crisis? How did you respond?
- What events in the life of your family have served to unexpectedly bring you closer together?
- How close are you to making peace with the children's biological mother? Is your answer related to the degree to which you feel *you're* a real mom?

* Chapter Twelve *

Stepping into the Future

You will find as you look back on your life that the moments when you have really lived are the moments when you have done things in a spirit of love.
—Henry Drummond

Our family's nightmare was far from over, and Larry and I were committed to doing whatever it took to help Elizabeth get well. It took plenty.

Elizabeth was hospitalized three times. Each October, she relapsed, was admitted into the hospital, and was discharged after varying lengths of time (from one to nearly three months). As a result, we spent three Thanksgivings, two Christmases, and a New Year's Eve in the eating disorder unit, fighting for her life.

We owe Elizabeth's recovery in no small part to her boyfriend, Zach (aka "Mr. Class Act," who stood by her through every painful step), the steadfast determination of her treatment team, and the love and prayers of many faithful friends. Their support enabled us to press on when we thought our nightmare would never end.

Today the disorder is held at bay. Elizabeth is tackling graduate school, and Larry and I are enjoying retirement together. As a testimony to our vow of harmony, we are united in joy as we celebrate Elizabeth's engagement and make plans for a beautiful wedding where we will officially welcome Zach into our family. We take each day as it comes, strangely grateful for the growth that was made possible by battling and surviving years of one mini-crisis after another capped by the most difficult crisis of all. Sometimes it takes such a tragedy for strong-willed people to pull together and unite properly as a family, but we knew God was with us, guiding our steps. Adversity made our relationship richer, our love deeper, and our lives fuller than ever before.

I would much rather that Elizabeth hadn't ever had to battle anorexia and that our family never had to go through that pain. Yet I keep thinking back to one of the verses that kept me going through the years of growing pains: "Be anxious for nothing, but in everything by prayer and supplication with thanksgiving let your requests be made known to God. And the peace of God, which surpasses all comprehension, will guard your hearts and your minds in Christ Jesus" (Philippians 4:6-7). So many times I had been granted peace by taking all my anxieties to the One who could handle them. Yet what were the words that immediately preceded Paul's admonition not to be anxious? "Rejoice in the Lord always; again I will say, rejoice!" (Philippians 4:4).

So while I would have spared our family the agony if I could have, I choose to rejoice. Our family rejoices together. We rejoice in the fact that we have each other, that we survived, and that seemingly against all odds we are still together.

Yes, our family began as grimly as Cinderella's story. Elizabeth and I each fancied herself the princess, and we both placed the other in the "wicked" role—leaving poor Prince Larry at his wit's end. We now know we were wrong; no one was wicked, but we were both misunderstood.

Have you been there? Maybe you are there right now, and if so, take heart. Cinderellas and stepmothers can work through their differences. Life is not a fairytale, and you can write your own ending. We have renounced our rivalry, and the word *wicked* has disappeared from Elizabeth's description of me. On Mother's Day, my card from my daughter describes feelings so tender I dash for a hankie. Our story concludes as a proper story should: "They lived happily ever after."

Our wish is the same for you.

> *We went through fire and through water,*
> *Yet You brought us out into a place of abundance.*
> —PSALM 66:12

Notes

1. Mrs. Charles E. Cowman, *Streams in the Desert* (Grand Rapids, Mich.: Zondervan, 1966), p. 71.
2. Bette Davis as quoted in *Simpson's Contemporary Quotations*, comp. James B. Simpson, 1988, www.bartleby.com/63/23/3623.html.
3. The Dixie Chicks, "Wide Open Spaces," copyright 1998, Sony Music Entertainment Inc./1997, 1998 Sony Music Entertainment, Inc./ Manufactured by Sony Music Entertainment Inc./550 Madison Avenue, NY, NY 10022-3211.

About the Authors

KALI SCHNIEDERS is a popular inspirational speaker who reaches out to hundreds of audiences by combining warmth, humor, and divine wisdom into touching stories and encouraging every generation to strive for their personal best. In her book *Truffles from Heaven*, Kali points out the spiritual significance that can be found in everyday moments. She was featured in *A Celebration of Women* alongside Elizabeth Dole, Mother Teresa, Shirley Dobson, Beth Moore, Anne Graham-Lotz, and Joyce Meyer. Kali currently lives in Dallas with her husband, Larry, and their fox terrier, Angel (aka Devil Dog).

ELIZABETH SCHNIEDERS graduated in 2003 from the University of Kansas with degrees in psychology and journalism. In her spare time, she enjoys running, cooking, and attempting to play tennis and golf (which you wouldn't expect after reading about her childhood experiences). She currently lives in Colorado, where she is pursuing her MBA at the University of Denver. She is also happily engaged to Zach, her college sweetheart.

We want to hear from you! E-mail us with questions or comments:

Kali: kali@astepmom.com
Elizabeth: elizabeth@astepmom.com

For speaking inquiries, please call
(972) 713-9070 or (214) 924-1291.

And please visit our website! www.astepmom.com

MORE WISDOM AND ENCOURAGEMENT FOR WOMEN.

The Purse-Driven Life

Anita Renfroe pulls no punches as she gives women an ultimatum: hilarity or insanity? This collection of estrogen-driven essays takes a look at a woman's "mid-life" (mid-section, mid-kids, mid-crazy) through a comedic grid.

Anita Renfroe   1-57683-605-3

Growing by Heart

Beautifully designed, this garden-themed devotional encourages women and teaches them how to memorize Scripture. Contains over one hundred different pullout Scripture memory cards arranged into fifty-two sections.

Scharlotte Rich   1-57683-683-5

Mothers Have Angel Wings

This special collection of stories will inspire, encourage, and challenge mothers as it explores specific biblical truths and how they relate to being a mom.

Carol Kent   1-57683-001-2

Secrets of a Mid-Life Mom

A first-time mother in her mid thirties, Jane speaks from the heart about being a new mom after thirty-five—and keeping a vigorous sense of humor! Jane encourages moms of all ages to enjoy every challenging minute of motherhood.

Jane Jarrell   1-57683-458-1

To order copies, visit your local Christian bookstore,
call NavPress at 1-800-366-7788, or log on to www.navpress.com.
To locate a Christian bookstore near you,
call 1-800-991-7747.

NAVPRESS ®
BRINGING TRUTH TO LIFE
www.navpress.com